The
Cotswold
Cottage

Trevor Yorke

COUNTRYSIDE BOOKS
NEWBURY BERKSHIRE

COUNTRYSIDE BOOKS
3 Catherine Road
Newbury
Berkshire
RG14 7NA

To view our complete range of books, please visit us at
www.countrysidebooks.co.uk

First published in 2015 by Countryside Books
Text © 2015 Trevor Yorke
Photos and illustrations © 2015 Trevor Yorke

A CIP record for this book is available from the British Library.

ISBN 978 1 84674 333 7

Produced by The Letterworks Ltd., Reading
Typeset by KT Designs, St Helens
Printed by Berforts Information Press, Oxford

CONTENTS

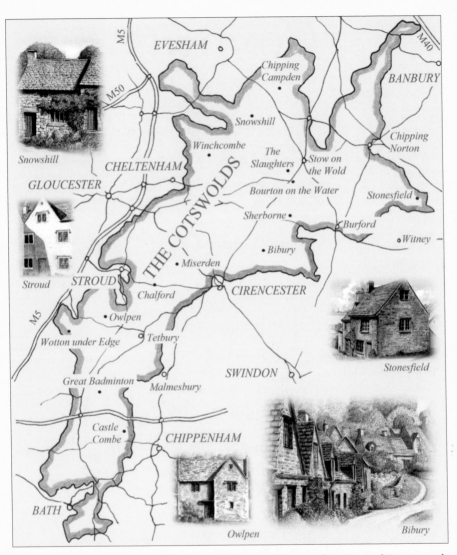

The map shows the following locations:

M5, EVESHAM, M50, Chipping Campden, BANBURY, M40, Snowshill, Snowshill, Winchcombe, The Slaughters, Stow on the Wold, Chipping Norton, CHELTENHAM, THE COTSWOLDS, Bourton on the Water, Stonesfield, GLOUCESTER, Sherborne, Burford, Witney, Bibury, Miserden, Stroud, STROUD, Chalford, CIRENCESTER, M5, Owlpen, Tetbury, Wotton under Edge, SWINDON, Great Badminton, Malmesbury, Stonesfield, Castle Combe, CHIPPENHAM, BATH, Owlpen, Bibury

This map shows the extent of the Cotswold Area of Outstanding Natural Beauty and some of the towns and villages mentioned in this book. The limestone hills which provide the distinctive stone for the region's cottages extend further south and north east. There are villages in these areas which share characteristics with those in the Cotswolds and they have also been included.

Introduction

There are few places in the country where the most attractive of cottages are set in such idyllic countryside. Glowing stone walls and rustic slate roofs, punctuated by dormers and chimneys, create rows of buildings full of movement and intrigue. The Cotswold villages, where these cottages are a vital ingredient, are often blessed with crystal clear streams, ancient greens and winding lanes which enhance the pastoral scene. Behind them, a patchwork of fields and rich woodland line the steep-sided valleys which enclose and envelope the buildings below.

The beauty of Cotswold cottages runs deeper than just an attractive view. The materials they are made of reflect the local landscape with colours and textures of stone that make the buildings appear to have been hewn out of the land rather than just planted upon it. Their character will have been determined by changes in local industry and farming as well as the properties of the materials used. Even the details like the tiny hinged windows, old planked doors and ironwork fittings were usually formed by local hands and have a style unique to the area.

Although this visual delight is celebrated in this book, there is also a focus on what lies under the skin of Cotswold cottages. How old are they, why were they built, and for whom?

How were they constructed and what are the problems you may face if you own one? What did they look like inside, and how was the garden used in the past? With an easy to understand text and my own drawings and photos I try to answer these questions, to make this a practical and informative guide for both the casual observer and cottage owner alike.

The book is divided into chapters describing the five key characteristics which define cottages; their form, the materials they are made from, their details, the interiors and colourful gardens. Chapter 1 outlines the history of the region and how the form and plan of cottages has changed through the ages. Chapter 2 describes the materials the walls and roofs are made from, how they are used and the problems owners may face with them. The next chapter looks at the details, from windows and doors to chimneys and porches, with tips on key areas of maintenance. Chapter 4 steps inside and describes the appearance of the cottage in the past. The final chapter explores the land around the building, how it was used by previous generations and what makes an ideal cottage garden today. There is a list of places to visit and a glossary explaining some of the less familiar terms.

Trevor Yorke

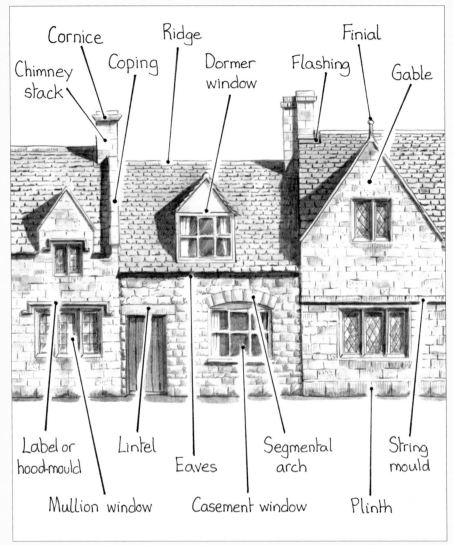

Chimney stack

Cornice

Coping

Ridge

Dormer window

Flashing

Finial

Gable

Label or hood-mould

Lintel

Eaves

Segmental arch

String mould

Mullion window

Casement window

Plinth

Cotswold cottages *with labels highlighting some of their key features.*

What is a Cottage?

If asked to visualise a cottage I think most of us would imagine a quaint, thatched building surrounded by a flower garden and a picket fence. However, take a look through a cottage holiday brochure or website and you will find all manner of buildings labelled as cottages. Some are tiny and tucked away in hamlets, while others are large, sprawling structures in seaside towns. Their age can be just as varied, with Tudor timber-framed houses vying with Victorian brick structures for your attention, some of which seem to stretch the definition to the limits. For the purposes of this book we first need to clarify the type of building we will be looking at.

A cottage is principally a small house set in a village. However, there are many Cotswold cottages in old towns which stagnated during the industrial revolution and have retained a village feel. Others were built for weavers and although they appear to be substantial, their living quarters were compact and fall within the remit of this book. The cottage would have originally been basically a single-storey building with one or two living rooms downstairs and bedrooms above, set partly within the roof and lit by small dormer windows. In many cases these have been extended upwards and outwards over the years so the cottage today can be quite a sizeable residence and certainly no longer justifying the label, single-storey. Whatever changes have been made, the cottage still needs to retain a rustic charm, weathered by time and complementing the surroundings rather than imposing itself upon them.

Another focus of this book is how cottages were built in the vernacular style, that is, using methods and materials from the local area. Up until the second half of the 19th century, when the railways made it easy to use

■ The word cottage is derived from the Old English 'cot' or 'cote' meaning a hut. It was the home of a cotter or cottager, just one of the tiers of peasantry within the medieval feudal system. At this time any reference to a cottage would have meant a small-holding including barns or sheds, not just the dwelling. From the 17th century the term came to refer to a small house, and it was only from the late 19th century that cottages were seen as attractive and desirable. Until then it had been a rather derogatory term.

cheaper, mass-produced bricks, slates and tiles from further afield, the cottage would have been built using local materials, extracted from the surrounding countryside. Their form and appearance were shaped by the properties of these materials and the traditional methods used by local builders.

These attributes are clearly displayed in old towns and villages in the parts of Gloucestershire and Oxfordshire which straddle the limestone belt and form the Cotswolds. Although much of what is described in this book will be useful to those interested in cottages in neighbouring counties like Wiltshire and Northamptonshire, there are some details and styles which are unique to this formerly remote and isolated upland area. In the beautiful wooded valleys that cut through the plateau, and along the crystal clear streams that burst out of the escarpment, nestle seemingly timeless villages with a wealth of cottages waiting to be discovered.

A selection of Cotswold cottages displaying the distinctive vernacular form which will be covered in this book. Despite their ancient appearance most will have been built from the late 17th to the early 19th century, with only a few of earlier origin. Some may have non-vernacular features such as sash windows but on the whole they are distinctive of this area, modest in their original size and rural in aspect.

CHAPTER 1

The Cottage Through Time

From peasants' hovels to Arts and Crafts homes

FIG 1.1: SNOWSHILL, GLOS: *Rambling cottages with richly textured ochre and grey stone walls and roofs, set against a backdrop of deep, wooded valleys are a hallmark of Cotswold villages. How did idyllic scenes like the one above develop? How old are the cottages and who were they built for?*

The Cotswolds is a unique and distinctive region that has been shaped by its geology, agriculture and industrial past. It has many characteristics in common with highland areas further north, such as stone walls, sheep farming and the old weaving industry. Yet at the same time

FIG 1.2: BURFORD, OXON: *A key feature of Cotswold towns is that away from the industrious south-west corner they largely bypassed the building boom of the late 19th and early 20th century. As a result, along their approach roads and down their back streets you can still find cottages that are often hundreds of years old.*

FIG 1.3: LOWER SLAUGHTER, GLOS: *Streams and small rivers were a magnet for settlement in the valleys below the escarpment, and villages seem rather incomplete without their clear bubbling waters. One of the finest examples is in Lower Slaughter where cottages, houses and old mills stand either side of the River Eye.*

■ Not all visitors to the Cotswolds have been enthusiastic about the area. William Cobbett (1763-1835) crossed this hilly region a number of times during his tours in the 1820s and described it as 'a very poor, dull, and uninteresting country'. The Revd F.E. Witts who lived in the Cotswolds around the same time called Chipping Campden 'a dull, clean, disused market town'. The change in attitude came about later in the century, as a new generation of visitors revelled in the picturesque setting and rusticated buildings which had failed to inspire earlier commentators.

it is influenced by surrounding lowland counties as its villages are dominated by country estates, manor houses and, since the last century, by the effects of tourism and commuting.

Travelling across the plateau for the first time can be disappointing, with the endless miles of large fields and bands of trees which dominate the landscape. However, it comes as a pleasant surprise when you turn off onto a back road to discover a picture-postcard scene of rustic buildings set along winding lanes, sparkling streams and old village greens. Some of these places are so familiar to us from film and

FIG 1.4: CASTLE COMBE, WILTS:
These old stone cottages with a busy roofline of pointed gables and chimneys, all set in a timeless, secluded valley make this one of the most picturesque English villages.

television that it almost feels as though you are about to come face to face with a film star.

However, the real stars of the show are the cottages. Seemingly positioned by an artist rather than a builder to create a pleasing visual effect, the stepped roof lines, miniature windows and glowing masonry evoke a deep rooted passion for the past. These humble homes have a varied history which is often not as ancient as it first appears to be. Many were created in recent centuries for select estate labourers or those working in the wool industry, while older cottages may have been converted from trade premises or the larger homes of wealthier villagers. Some were planned and built as part of

a new village, complete with gardens and landscaping. Others were scattered over whatever land was available. Whatever the age of the cottages, their purpose and form was shaped by circumstances and changes in the local countryside. We therefore begin our exploration of these limestone-walled gems by looking briefly at the events which brought them into being.

Late Medieval Cottages
The pattern of settlement on the Cotswold plateau, with a few small villages nestling in the valleys below, is largely a result of sheep farming. Wool from the area was in great demand across Europe during the medieval period. Areas were cleared and villages abandoned, especially on land owned by the monasteries, to make sheep farming more profitable. Despite the dominance of abbeys, a significant quantity of fleeces came from peasants with small flocks and a number of merchants made their fortune by selling the wool from these smaller producers.

The cottage emerges on documents at this time as a small holding rather than just a small house. It was lower in status than larger farms and the manor itself, but it included land so the tenant could feed his family. In some cases the lord of the manor gave permission for a cottage to be built within the village, or it could have formed part of a new area like a medieval version of a modern housing estate. In other settlements it could be built upon waste or common land, the general rule being that you had to have a fire burning in the grate by the morning after you started building for you to gain the right to stay (a statute of 1589 ended the legal right of a peasant to do this but it was not always imposed so the practice often continued).

Much of the peasant housing from this period would have only stood for a few generations as tenants could not afford to pay for a builder and materials would have been limited to whatever they were allowed to gather.

Stone was expensive to extract so was used only for the finer buildings. Peasants may have been able to collect some from fields but it would have been just sufficient to form a base. The walls and roof were usually made of more readily available timber and straw. The medieval cottage would have been a long single-storey structure with low walls and a large thatched roof, accompanied by a scattering of outbuildings. In many there was an

Living area

Cross passage

Byre

FIG 1.5: MEDIEVAL COTTAGES: *Although there has been little excavation and study of medieval cottages within the Cotswolds, it is assumed from the footprint they have left in deserted villages that they took a similar form to the building pictured here. These longhouses accommodated both a peasant farmer's family and their livestock, and varied in size depending upon the status of the occupant. Despite this being stone country it is likely that most of these buildings had timber frames and were covered in lime wash and thatch, with limestone restricted to the plinth that the building stood on.*

internal division which separated a room for the family to eat and sleep in from another space occupied by livestock.

None of the peasants' cottages from this period survive today. All you are likely to find are raised rectangular platforms resulting from generations of rebuilding showing where a cottage once stood. There are a small number of medieval houses which we might today describe as cottages but these were the homes of people of higher status, or they were buildings associated with the wool trade which

FIG 1.6: MEDIEVAL WARWICK ALMSHOUSES, BURFORD, OXON:
The medieval houses which survive in the Cotswolds were associated with wool merchants, the monasteries or they were the humble abode of a priest. A few of today's cottages began life as this better class of home. With stone walls and carved doorways they would have been of a superior quality to the hovels around them. Only later did they drop in status due to their limited size and unfashionable style. These almshouses dating from the 1450s contain arched details typical of medieval buildings.

have later been divided in order to make smaller homes.

Late 16th to Early 18th-Century Cottages

During this period the Cotswolds bore witness to significant changes. The imposition of higher taxes on exports made English wool less attractive to foreign weavers and the emphasis changed to the production of woven cloth, an industry which eventually became centred in the south-western corner of the region around Stroud. Weavers' cottages were erected on common land above the fulling mills in the valley, creating new settlements that seemed to cling to the hillsides.

When the monasteries were dissolved in the 1530s their estates were snapped up by wealthy courtiers and locals, or they were split up to create opportunities for a new breed of yeoman farmers. The peasants who once owed services to the lord of the manor in return for certain rights now became tenants and paid labourers. With the creation of the Church of England, the rich no longer pumped money into ecclesiastical building programmes to ensure a safe passage to heaven but sought glory on a more earthly scale by building themselves new fashionable country houses, especially in the period from 1580-1630. The financial benefits of an improving national economy, and the local trade in wool and cloth in particular worked their way down the social ladder so that weavers, quarrymen and even labourers could find themselves in small stone houses.

This is the period when the

distinctive Cotswold cottage begins to appear in villages and towns across the region. They were typically compact structures with just one or two ground-floor rooms and a sleeping space under the eaves. Part of the reason why Cotswold buildings look so old is that these new cottages, which were built during the 17th century, were using design features found on late medieval

FIG 1.7: LATE 16TH/EARLY 17TH CENTURY: *The distinctive Cotswold cottage is a creation of the late 16th and 17th centuries, as in these examples in Burford (top) and Stanton (bottom). The gables above the eaves, stone mullion windows and projecting label moulds above the openings persisted in the Cotswolds well into the 18th century. One improvement over their medieval predecessors was the fireplace and chimney, which meant that an upper floor could be inserted and rooms created in the roof space.*

FIG 1.8: MIDDLE STREET, STROUD, LATE 17TH CENTURY: *Weavers' cottages began to appear in the Stroud area as the woollen industry boomed. Some were quite large, as in this example with two main storeys and a third set in the roof as a working space. A single full height central gable with a mullion and a small oval window above (to light a high storage space) is distinctive of these buildings.*

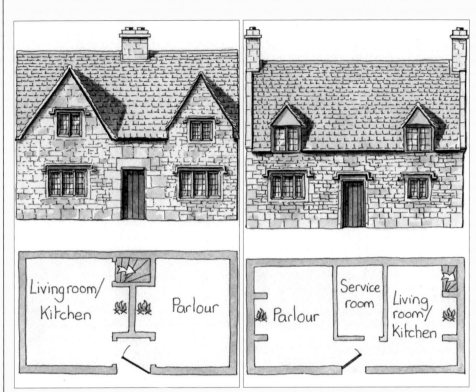

FIG 1.9: 17TH CENTURY COTTAGES: *The plan of cottages in the 17th century was shaped by rising expectations, a desire to create a roughly symmetrical facade and the inclusion of fireplaces and chimneys. They could range from a single ground floor space which served as a living room and kitchen, with a bedroom in the loft above (FIG 1.7 top) to a row of three ground floor rooms for a yeoman. Many of these still had a medieval-style cross passage to give direct access between the front and rear of the property. A popular design for a better class of cottage was the lobby entrance plan (top left) in which the central door opens into a small lobby in front of the fireplace with a compact staircase on the other side. This could have two rooms as shown here or an additional third unheated space at one end. These can be identified on the outside by a large central chimney stack in line with the front door. Another type from the late 17th century which can be found in the Cotswolds had fireplaces in the gable end walls with an additional central unheated service room which could be used as a work space or for storage (top right). Many of these simple plans were later extended with the addition of an outshot at the back (low rooms under an extension of the main roof). Despite the appearance of these permanent homes there were still many peasants living in older ramshackle hovels which would only be replaced in the following century.*

houses rather than being influenced by the latest fashions. They had triangular gables along their facades, hood moulds draped above openings in the wall, tall chimneys and stone mullion windows. The development of permanent quarries during the 17th century meant that limestone roof tiles became available. These necessitated a steep pitched roof which is another distinctive feature of the region's houses.

Georgian and Victorian

It is likely that the majority of cottages we see in the Cotswolds today date from the 18th and 19th centuries. Increased agricultural output and the short-lived boom in the woollen industry from the 1790s to 1830s, created a need to house skilled craftsmen and labourers. Some cottages were built in estate villages as pairs or rows, others were placed in short terraces close to mills and quarries.

■ THE WOOL INDUSTRY

The wool industry began to shape the character of the Cotswolds before the Norman Conquest. The dry, open plateau was ideal for keeping sheep with only shepherds required to look after them and the villages in the valleys below burst into life when the flocks were brought down to be washed or sheered. By the end of the 15th century the monarchy had increased taxation on the export of wool to such an extent that merchants from the continent began buying up the locally-produced woollen cloth which bypassed the levy. This industry became concentrated in the mills on the fast flowing streams around Stroud, peaking in the late 18th and early 19th century before competition from the large mills in the north of the country brought about a decline in this local trade.

The woollen cloth industry in the 17th and 18th centuries was largely controlled by wealthy clothiers. They bought the raw wool then sent it out on packhorse or cart to families in local cottages. Here it could be cleaned, carded and then spun on a spinning wheel before being woven into cloth on a loom (the equipment was often rented out to the weaver by the clothier). The cloth was then taken to a fulling mill where it was pounded in water to felt it up and shrink it before it was hung out to dry in the surrounding fields. The clothier owned the material rights and made his profit from the sale of this finished cloth, the men and women who had created it were only paid a small fee for their efforts. Cottages were often erected by the weavers themselves with help from family and neighbours. They would try and site them on common land below the cold hilltops but above the fulling mills and cloth-drying fields in the valley below. Although some weavers' cottages look reasonably spacious today we should remember that they had to accommodate looms, spinning wheels and other equipment and materials before they could make room for their often large families.

FIG 1.10: GEORGIAN PERIOD:
A selection of mid and late-18th-century cottages from the Bibury area. Gables along the facade and stone mullion windows were now rare (bottom), most had cheaper and more compact dormer windows set in the roof (top left) or a low upper storey (top right) with wooden casement windows. The hood moulds over the openings disappeared as guttering became more common, and cheaper timber (top right) or dressed stone (bottom) lintels became plain and flush with the walls. Symmetry was more prevalent by this date, with windows neatly in line and the door roughly central (top left and bottom).

FIG 1.11: BLAISE HAMLET, BRISTOL, THE PICTURESQUE MOVEMENT:

From the second half of the 18th century, many architects and their aristocratic clients became influenced by the picturesque movement, creating whimsical, rustic buildings and setting them so they appeared to have been plucked from a painting. It was on lesser estate buildings where they experimented with these ideas, using materials in their natural form, with irregularly shaped plans and distressed finishes. Old cottages became models for the design of estate workers' houses, as with these examples designed by John Nash in what was known as the Cottage Orné style. Pattern books were produced with a variety of designs intended to complement a gentleman's country residence, and they were used throughout the following century for estate cottages. These were not always acts of benevolence by the owners, more often they were meant to enliven the approach to the large house to impress guests.

FIG 1.12: CHIPPING CAMPDEN, GLOS, VICTORIAN PERIOD:

This classically styled mid-19th-century terrace looks rather grand with string courses between the floors and dressings around the doors and windows. However this is a row of four cottages, each with a small single room on three floors (the lighter stonework highlights a single cottage). With such limited width, the front doors were offset. The symmetry which was key in classical architecture, was achieved by spacing the windows out evenly along the upper floors. This type of narrow cottage can be found in cloth-making areas like Stroud.

■ THE REALITY OF LIVING IN A VICTORIAN COTTAGE

Despite being visually picturesque, many 19th-cottages were appalling to live in. Decline in the woollen industry and the loss of common land after enclosure had left many struggling to make a living. By 1840, weavers were working up to 16 hours a day for as little as 5 shillings (25p) a week. Most had to supplement their poor wage with piecework while women and children laboured in the fields or carried out a local craft. Richard Heath used his 1893 book *The English Peasant* to catalogue the true state of rural labourers' homes as found by health officials over the previous decades.

He describes some cottages as 'crazy, dilapidated hovels, shaking with every wind', while inspectors found many cottages 'tumbledown and ruinous, not water-tight, very deficient in bedroom accommodation, and indecent sanitary arrangements'. It was stated in parts of Gloucestershire that bedrooms were found with children sleeping on pillows soaked wet by rain pouring in through a leaky roof. A policeman in the Stroud area commented that 'they are wretchedly off in bedding; there are many cases where the man and his wife and as many as 7 children have slept on straw laid on the floor with only a torn quilt to cover them'. It is little surprise then that there was an exodus of the labouring class from the Cotswolds during this period.

FIG 1.13: DESIGN OF ESTATE COTTAGES: *These examples from Sherborne (left) and Stanway (right) were a significant improvement on the hovels most labourers lived in. From the late 18th century, authors of pattern books designed compact but well built estate cottages with only one or two rooms on each floor. The style often replicated that of 17th-century Cotswold cottages. Early examples were just in pairs or short rows but by the 1830s, when Sherborne was laid out, they were often part of larger schemes.*

FIG 1.14: GREAT BADMINTON, GLOS, GOTHIC REVIVAL ARCHITECTURE: *By the mid 19th century most estate cottages in the region reflected national styles although they were mostly still being built with local stone. These, dating from 1860, have decorative bargeboards and latticework glazing bars in the windows, both fashionable Gothic details from the Victorian period.*

FIG 1.15: GEORGIAN AND VICTORIAN TERRACES: *The majority of stone cottages which stand today in the Cotswolds date from the 18th and 19th centuries. Single-cell cottages with one room on the ground floor and a ladder or steps leading up to a bedroom (left), were common in the 18th century. When built into a slope they usually had the fireplace in the wall, which was dug into the ground to help combat damp. These can be found not only along streets and lanes, but built in rows at the back of urban houses. By the 19th century, larger versions with one and a half (right) or two ground floor rooms and taller bedrooms above were being built. This gave extra space for a pantry, larder or work area, with separate bedrooms upstairs. In general these terraced cottages become gradually taller and deeper with short extensions at the rear by the turn of the 20th century.*

Development of the Victorian Cottage

The traditional form of Cotswold cottage lasted into the early 18th century after which the design began to be influenced by architectural pattern books and more general trends in building. The rows of gables along the facade were the first to go, being replaced by smaller dormer windows set into the roof. Drip moulds above windows became rare by the middle of the century with simple timber lintels and, later, shallow stone arches taking their place. The old stone mullion windows were superseded by wooden casements around the same time. The Georgian cottage was more orderly and where possible symmetrical, but with the continued use of local stone they still fitted in seamlessly with older buildings of the village.

Despite the Victorian period being viewed as a glorious industrial and commercial success there were areas, like the Cotswolds, which were bypassed by many of its benefits. The woollen industry was in decline and by the second half of the 19th century many once-busy towns were showing signs of disuse with workers leaving for more prosperous parts of the country. The enclosure of parishes during the previous century in the name of agricultural improvement created the neatly walled fields and straight roads which characterise much of the region and often gave the landowners the opportunity to control those who lived and worked on their estates. The more desirable staff could be housed in finely built cottages complementing the country house they served; others were simply forced out, and deprived of the common land their livestock once grazed. It was in the interests of local landowners to remove these people from the village to lessen their contribution to the poor rate, until the Union Chargeability Act of 1865 grouped parishes together to reduce this practice.

Larger estate villages, built with a distinct style often reviving the appearance of 17th-century cottages, are a feature of the Victorian period in the Cotswolds. By the second half of the 19th century homes could be built with brick and Welsh slate as the railways brought cheaper mass-produced materials to the region.

During the rural decline of the late 19th century artists and architects suddenly became interested in cottages. Paintings of rustic, tumbledown houses framed by tall trees and rose gardens

■ DATING COTTAGES

It always pays to look down the side or along the rear of a building. The front may have been rebuilt to present a more fashionable façade but the other walls were often left or were built with cheaper materials. Evidence can sometimes be seen of how a cottage has been extended with, perhaps, a change in stonework down the side, or the marks left by a neighbouring property now removed.

FIG 1.16: THE FLOOR PLAN: *A large cottage typical of those built in rural areas during the first half of the 19th century. Although it has a plain façade it still uses casement windows and is built with local stone. They could be of a single room depth with one positioned either side of the front door or they could be double piled, with one room behind another, as was common in urban areas.*

became fashionable, they represented an idealised rural past which had a strong appeal in this rapidly industrialising age. At the same time they recorded the dilapidated state many of them were in, as behind the charming façade were homes with leaking roofs, damp walls, worn out windows and doors, and little in the way of drainage or water supplies.

The picturesque villages of the Cotswolds also attracted artists and craftsmen who planned to do more than just create paintings. Working under the broad banner of the Arts and Crafts movement they established guilds and communities which helped revive old skills and created work for locals and outsiders alike. They helped attract others of a similar persuasion to come and restore old houses and cottages, and save buildings for future generations.

FIG 1.17: CHIPPING CAMPDEN, GLOS: *It is a bit of a surprise today, within neatly trimmed Cotswold towns and villages, to find unrestored cottages like this compact example which probably dates from the early 19th century.*

FIG 1.18: UPPER SLAUGHTER, GLOS, THE ARTS AND CRAFTS MOVEMENT:
This movement was led by groups of craftsmen, artists and architects who sought to revive traditional working methods, using local materials, and create a medieval social order in response to the ills they saw in the factory system. It was a socialist movement inspired by the writings of Victorian art critic John Ruskin and the work of designer William Morris. Although their view of the past was rather rose-tinted those working under the banner of the movement created some of the finest pieces of art and architecture from the late 19th and early 20th centuries. They established an appetite for the restoration of old buildings and inspired modernist as well as traditional architecture.

The Cotswolds became a centre for the Arts and Crafts movement. Morris had long lived at Kelmscott, near Lechlade. Ernest Gimson, and Sidney and Ernest Barnsley established themselves in Sapperton while C.R. Ashbee moved his Guild of Handicraft from London to Chipping Campden in 1902. Other notable designers like Norman Jewson, F.L.Griggs, Dietmer Blow and Edwin Lutyens, who rebuilt the cottages pictured here, all worked in the region. The very nature of their subtle restoration work means the cottages do not stand out as clear pieces of inventive architecture as their larger houses did. Instead it is through the detail, like long mullion windows with four or five lights and steep sloping buttresses, that their work can be identified (see also FIG 3.20)

CHAPTER 2

Cottage Materials

Limestone, Stone Slates and Thatch

FIG 2.1: STONESFIELD, OXON: *Cotswold limestone has long been used for building, but large-scale quarrying and construction of cottages only began in the 17th century. In some areas the rock splits into flat slates which are used to make distinctive roofs such as those in Stonesfield where this row of cottages stands.*

The geology of the region directly shapes the appearance of its cottages. Not only does it give them the warm stone walls and rustic roof tiles which are so distinctive of the Cotswolds but it determines where the towns and villages are sited, the nature of its agriculture and industry, and also the remoteness which has helped maintain its regional character. The limestone which covers most of the upland area is porous, allowing water to drain through until it reaches a layer of clay where it is forced out at the sides of valleys and the escarpment as springs which attract human settlement. The dry hilltops and plateau were only useful for sheep farming on a large scale, and it was this industry that paid for and shaped the appearance of cottages. Finally the barrier of the escarpment kept canals, main-line railways and motorways at bay preserving the Cotswolds in the modern age.

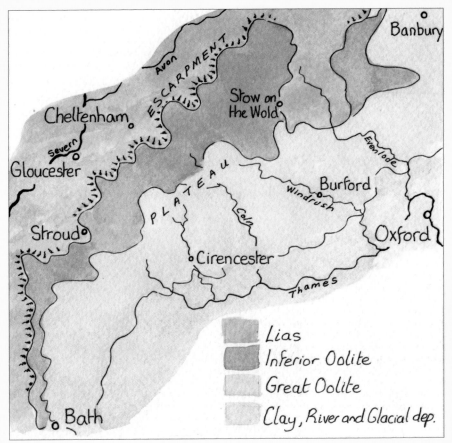

FIG 2.2: LIMESTONE: *A simplified map showing the limestone belt which forms the underlying rock of most of the Cotswolds. The principal building stones are in the bands of inferior and great oolitic limestone. Below this are the lias stones which are exposed along the escarpment and run below the River Severn, and above are layers of clay, chalk, and glacial and river deposits. This sandwich was later tilted up in the west and erosion exposed the lower layers (see FIG 2.5).*

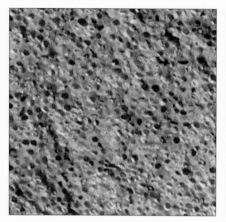

FIG 2.3: LIMESTONE BLOCK: *A close-up showing the tiny round spheres (ooliths) and the holes left by those which have fallen out.*

Limestone

The Cotswolds form part of a belt of limestone hills that run north-east from Dorset on the south coast, up through Gloucestershire and Oxfordshire, and eventually into Yorkshire. These were formed in shallow, clear Jurassic seas over 140 million years ago. Crustaceans fell to the seabed, their shells broke down and along with particles of sand and mud became coated in calcium carbonate to form tiny spheres. Over the millennia these built up in layers of fine, pale deposits. The materials in which these spheres were laid formed the cement which bound them together and gave the individual character to the local

FIG 2.4: LITTLE BARRINGTON, GLOS, LIMESTONE-TILED ROOFS:
Steeply-pitched, limestone-tiled roofs are a key characteristic of Cotswold cottages. Note the skirts around the base of the chimneys on this cottage, designed to throw water clear of the vulnerable junction with the roof tiles.

stone. Some of these layers were more suitable for building than others. The spheres can still be seen in Cotswold stone today as tiny dots. Early geologists thought they looked like fish roe known as ooliths so they called the rock oolitic limestone. Over time, the ancient seabed rose and fell and went through further phases of deposition and erosion, creating different layers, some of which can be used to help split the limestone into blocks when it is being quarried out.

Building with limestone

There are a number of ways in which the stone walls of buildings can be constructed. The cheapest method, which was widely used for cottage walls, made use of variously sized pieces of undressed stone to make mortared rubble walls. The stone could have been picked up from fields as well as taken from a village quarry. An inner and an outer skin were built up, with smaller stones mixed with clay forming a central core. In some walls an occasional through stone was used to run deep into the wall to help bind the faces together but it is rare in this region. Instead, the strength of the walls relies upon the larger, squared-off pieces (quoins) which form the corners and line the openings. In better quality buildings the stones were sorted and trimmed so they could be laid in neat courses with dressed stone used for the quoins and openings. Rangework used neatly squared-off stone blocks with finer joints, but was laid in courses.

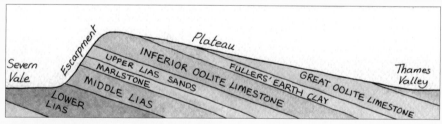

FIG 2.5: COTSWOLD GEOLOGY: *A much simplified section through the Cotswolds showing the sequence of rocks beneath. Notice how the layers have all been tilted so that erosion has exposed the lower layers along the plateau and escarpment. The lower lias which runs across the Severn Vale contains a very hard limestone used for paving slabs in the Cotswolds. Topping the middle lias is a band of marlstone, a sandy limestone which marks the point where springs emerge from the escarpment and valley sides. Marlstone was used for building in north Oxfordshire. The inferior oolite limestone which tops the escapement is so named because it lies beneath the great, not because it is of any lesser quality. In its lower and middle layers is some of the best building stone in the region including peagrit, yellow and white Guiting and Painswick stone. Above this is a band of fuller's earth, then the great oolitic limestone, much used in Bath. It is typically a hard and shelly stone and includes Hampton weatherstone, Taynton stone, Bath stone and cornbrash which disappears under the Oxford clay along the south-east edge of the region.*

FIG 2.6: COTSWOLD COLOURS: *The materials which formed the various types of oolitic limestone, and the conditions under which they were formed, will determine the texture, colour, strength and porosity of the stone. A high sand content will make the stone stronger, a large proportion of crystals adds durability, and those which are finely grained can be polished and are known as marbles. Softer limestone is often called marl and is not always suitable for building. Tiny quartz crystals make some stone sparkle, while an iron oxide called limonite is mainly responsible for the golden or rusty colour found in the north of the region. Where the influence of the iron oxide is strong, as in Northamptonshire, it is called*

ironstone. The cottages pictured here show how the colours can vary from greys in Painswick in the south (top left), to the warmer hues of Bibury (top right) and finally the rusty colours in the north of the region at Bloxham (bottom).

■ QUARRYING

Most villages and country estates would have had a small pit or quarry although cottage owners may not have had access to these. Commercial quarries existed in the medieval period, sited close to a river for easy transportation, those at Taynton near Burford are known to have supplied stone to Oxford and London. From the 17th century these became more widespread especially with improvements in transport and mechanised cutting machines in the 19th century. The stone could be extracted from above, worked out of seams on a quarry face, or be mined out. Quarrymen used picks to make a horizontal gap along a seam or crack to expose the top of a section of limestone. Then with saws they would cut down to form the blocks they intended to extract. As limestone is a sedimentary rock, chips and wedges could be inserted underneath each block so they would split along these planes. A lewis hole or pincers were used to pull the block free. While there was still a high moisture level in the stone (known as quarry sap) it could be easily cut into smaller pieces in any direction (a freestone). Later, as it dries, it forms a harder protective skin. Today most quarries have closed and restrictions on expansion of existing quarries or opening of new ones means it can be hard to source the exact stone which other conservation rules insist upon when carrying out building work.

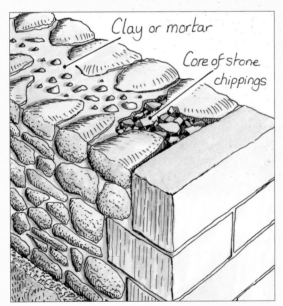

Clay or mortar

Core of stone chippings

FIG 2.7: A CUT THROUGH A RANDOM RUBBLE WALL: *The mortar not only helps hold the wall together but is also important to ensure that water does not penetrate and wash out the core.*

The stone blocks varied in height, sometimes with random blocks which spanned more than one course. The best walling, known as ashlar, used smooth dressed stone for the front of the house with joints so fine that only a thin layer of lime putty rather than mortar was used between the blocks. This was usually just a facing, with stone rubble (and later brick rubble) used to make up the wall behind. These cheaper materials are usually visible down the side and rear of the building. Today walls are constructed with a gap between them filled with insulation, and ties holding the outer and inner face together. Artificial stone (crushed stone and cement cast onto a concrete block) is typically used for the outer face of new houses and is better suited for use with modern cement mortars than real limestone.

Lime mortar was used between the stones principally to spread the load

FIG 2.8: EXAMPLES OF STONEWORK FROM COTSWOLD COTTAGES: *Most will be random rubble or roughly coursed (top line). Finer quality work (bottom line) can be found in some cottages but ashlar (bottom centre) might only be found on a few estate cottages. Machine cut rock-faced stone (bottom right) was popular in the late Victorian period. Note the random pitting on the corner stones in the top left image. This is to give render a good fix to the smooth stone (the rough random rubble would not require it) and shows that this building was probably rendered in the past.*

from the floors and roof above, and to seal the wall against the elements. Lime was an essential ingredient in the past as it also helped the mortar stick to bricks and stone, allowed moisture to escape, and it made the wall more tolerant of movement and less likely to crack. It was made by burning lumps of limestone in a kiln and extracting quicklime which was then mixed with water causing it to slake until only lime

putty was left. (When using quicklime today be sure to follow safety instructions as it can burn like acid.). The putty could be used in this form for the fine joints of ashlar walls but it was more often mixed with sand and water to make lime mortar. The surface was kept damp or covered to stop it drying too quickly and cracking.

FIG 2.9: LAYING THE STONE:
It is important that dressed stone is laid in the same direction as it was formed so that its natural layers are set horizontally, as in this example. Any water penetrating the gaps between the layers will not cause the stone to split because of the weight of the stone above pressing down. Where the face of stone has flaked away (delaminated) it is often because it has been face-bedded with the layers running vertically, so water can get behind each layer and as it freezes in winter and expands it pushes the layer away. The bedding is clear in this example.

■ FOUNDATIONS

Although we assume a cottage which has stood for centuries might be more substantially built than a modern house there are key areas where old houses lag behind. The value of good foundations for houses was not fully appreciated until the 20th century. Most cottages built before this time may have little more than the top soil removed creating a short ditch into which the wall was built up. As a result it is common for old buildings to sag or lean slightly, often due to the initial settlement. If there are no fresh signs of movement then it should not be of concern. However there can be changes to the local environment such as a rising water table, large trees and shrubs, paved or tarmac drives, increased road traffic and cracked drains, which can cause the ground to rise or fall to a greater degree than in the past. Houses built on clays like fuller's earth can be more prone to ground movement. If any fresh cracks appear in the walls then these should be investigated.

FIG 2.10: POINTING: *The way in which the mortar is finished, the pointing, varies. Originally, in random rubble walls, the mortar was spread out level with the face of the stone (left) as the surface was usually to be lime washed. Today, as the fashion is to leave the stone exposed, this patchy pointing does not look attractive so a neater finish which is slightly recessed or flush with the wall but with a slope to encourage rain to fall out, is preferable. Ribbon pointing (right) where a squared line of mortar projects from the wall is not traditional and can be a source of problems as it tends to trap water on its upper edge.*

■ CONDENSATION

The most common cause of damp and mould is condensation which occurs when air with a high moisture content hits a cold surface like a window or a solid exterior wall, making the water vapour condense into droplets. The black and green mould which appears most often in corners and behind furniture is fungus which thrives in damp cold conditions. In earlier times leaky windows, chimneys, wall vents and doors reduced humidity in a house but in the modern home these are often sealed. Moisture levels are increased through the use of tumble dryers, drying clothes inside and the production of a lot of steam in kitchens and bathrooms without adequate extraction. To reduce the level of mould try to leave windows open a crack when you are in, fit an extractor in kitchens and bathrooms, put tumble dryers in a garage or outbuilding and pull furniture away from an exterior wall. There are various systems available which remove excessive humidity, including desiccant dehumidifiers which are useful for drying clothes while keeping moisture levels low. The other approach is to warm the internal walls so the moisture does not condense. Leaving the heating on all day is not friendly to your pocket or the environment. The best approach is to insulate the walls, a time-consuming and disruptive job but one which can be done in phases and which will save you money on heating bills.

■ PROBLEMS WITH STONE WALLS

Although limestone is structurally strong there are a number of issues which can affect its appearance and the integrity of the walls it is used for. Over the past century cement-based mortars have often been used for repairing stone walls. As water cannot pass through this, moisture tends to build up within the stones. If this water freezes it expands and forces the outer surface of the stone to flake away. This is made worse if the stone has been face-bedded (see FIG 2.9). Many cement mortars contain salts which can leach out, staining the wall and causing damage to the stone itself (this can also happen where road salt is regularly splashed up against a wall). Cement mortars are more rigid than lime mortar and are prone to cracking if there is any slight movement in the walls. This can allow water to penetrate beyond the surface which can potentially damage the core if it is left unchecked. Grouts or lime and ash mixes can be injected into the centre of the wall if this is an issue. Stone can also suffer from the effects of acid rain, or damage sustained when it was quarried and even excessive droppings where pigeons and starlings gather. As a general rule limestone walls should be built and repaired using lime mortar (although some lime mortar mixes contain cement to accelerate setting).

Exterior walls can crack and bow due to poor building methods, problems with foundations or changes to the structure of a cottage like the installation of a new staircase which cuts through the horizontal tie beams. As Cotswold stone walls do not usually have through stones the outer leaf can also come away from the core creating a similar effect. In the past buttresses were built on the outside to check the movement, and more recently iron or steel rods have been installed beneath floorboards and fixed on the outside of opposing walls with metal discs, s shapes or cross straps to stop the movement (see FIG 2.11).

Damp is a regular problem with any solid wall. It is not necessarily a fault as a degree of moisture was always expected to be present. As the limestone, lime mortar and lime wash allowed the wall to breathe, any water within could evaporate away. In many cases it is later changes to this arrangement which have created a new problem. Masonry paints and silicon wall treatments may keep rain out but they also keep moisture in. Garden soil is sometimes left to build up against a wall and climbing plants can also cause problems. Leaky gutters, damaged flashing on the roof and gaps around openings in a wall can let water through (the damp patches inside may not be directly opposite these sources). High moisture levels can also be found in walls where salts left behind by periodic rising water absorb moisture from the air and indicate that there is a problem with rising damp. It is worth seeking expert advice if the damp is something you cannot tolerate. Interpreting the information, finding the source of the problem and a suitable remedy is not always straightforward and modern remedies are usually not suitable for traditional stone walls.

FIG 2.11: PROBLEMS WITH MOVEMENT: *A wall which is bowing out is held back by metal ties running under the floorboards and fixed to the cross-shaped metal plates on the outside.*

FIG 2.12: RENDER: *The majority of Cotswold cottages had their stone covered or washed over in the past. Rubble walls benefited from a protective coat so that rain would not penetrate. Mortar was spread out to smooth the outer surface of the wall (see FIG 2.10) and the whole was then coated with lime wash (lime putty mixed with water and milk to make a thin white paint) with numerous coats built up to get the*

desired finish. A pigment could be added for colour, popular choices were pastel tones and yellow ochre. Some cottages were rendered first with a lime mortar containing small stones and pebbles, known as roughcast, which was thrown at the wet wall to create a rough protective coat. In the 20th century the fashion was to remove render or not renew faded lime wash. Although the rustic stone creates a pleasing appearance, damp can enter through the wide mortar joints which were never originally meant to be exposed.

Since the late 19th century, cement-based mortars have been widely used. These are generally impervious to water and are stronger, complementing the properties of modern bricks and artificial stone. However when it comes to repairing stonework the use of cement mortars can often lead to problems as they trap moisture in the stone and contain elements which can damage the surface.

Brick

This is a rare material in the heart of the Cotswolds, and where brick

FIG 2.13: AN EARLY 19TH-CENTURY COTTAGE: *At first glance it appears to be built of limestone but a quick look down the side reveals a brick structure, the stone being a facing of approximately four inches thick. The checked pattern created by light-coloured headers in the red brickwork was fashionable in the Regency period.*

cottages are found they tend to date from the second half of the 19th century. There are however, a number of late Georgian and Victorian cottages which have a thin facing of limestone across the front of the structure, the remainder of which is made of brick. Before the railways brought in mass-produced bricks from around the country these building blocks were very much the vernacular, their colour and texture reflecting the nature of the local clay from which they were made and the firing method used. The oldest bricks tend to vary in size and will usually have a worn, rough finish, with thick lines of mortar. Varieties from the 18th and early 19th centuries are more regular and were set in a distinct pattern, while later mass-produced bricks usually have a consistent colour and are sharper edged. A useful tool to date bricks is a frog, the recess in the top and bottom, which was introduced in the early 19th century. Flat-surfaced bricks will usually date from before this.

A solid brick wall will have stretchers (a brick laid lengthways) on the inner and outer face between which the headers (with the short end exposed) are laid to hold the two sides together. The arrangement of these headers and stretchers in the brick wall is referred to as the bond. Flemish bond, with alternate headers and stretchers on each course, was dominant in the 18th and 19th centuries, English bond which had a course of headers followed by one of stretchers was widely used in the 16th and 17th centuries and was revived in the late 19th century although these tended to use a large number of bricks so it was common in cottages and terraces for a few courses of stretchers to be used before a row containing headers to save on cost.

Timber framing

The construction of a large framework of timber, with the gaps filled with wattle and daub, was the standard method of building for late-medieval houses in this region. Although some wealthy individuals could afford stone, most masons were busy building for the Crown and Church, whereas skilled carpenters were more readily available. However, by the 16th century good timber was becoming scarce and with the dissolution of the monasteries, church building virtually ground to a

FIG 2.14: CASTLE COMBE, WILTS: *Some original timber framed houses were built on top of a stone lower storey, as in this example. You cannot always assume that cottages which appear like the example pictured here were always as originally built. It was common practice in some areas during the 18th and 19th centuries to fully or partially cover up old timber framed houses with more fashionable materials like stone.*

halt, so masons could turn to secular building. The emerging classical style of architecture made stone fashionable, and the fire risk associated with timber meant that good quality timber-framed houses became rare after this period. Cottages built from timber could have originally been higher status homes which had become unfashionable and slipped down the social scale, or were former farm houses which had been split up to form labourers' homes at a later date. There are some original timber-framed cottages, mainly around the edge of the region, which have survived. Although, like their larger contemporaries, they are often faced with stone so the timbers are not visible at the front, or they have had their infill replaced by brick.

FIG 2.15: STRUCTURE OF TIMBER FRAMING: *There are two principal forms of timber-framed house. The most common is made with a grid of vertical posts and horizontal beams which make a square structure called box framing. Older examples tend to have large panels with thick timbers. Tightly spaced vertical posts called close studding was popular in the 16th century, while later or cheaper buildings had thinner pieces of widely spaced timbers. An alternative method, called cruck framing, used pairs of slightly bent timbers connected at the top to make triangular frames. They were set in rows of three or more with lesser timbers fixed off this to make the outer wall, as in this example in Didbrook in Gloucestershire. These are rare and often older than surviving box framed buildings.*

ROOFING MATERIALS
Stone slates

The Cotswold area is fortunate in not only having good building stone for walls, but also outcrops which can form thin sheets suitable for roofing. It is these roughly textured limestone slabs which give cottages in the region their distinctive form (they are called tiles in the south of the region while slates is the more usual term in the north). There are only a handful of places where the appropriate stone can be found, most notably near Stonesfield in Oxfordshire where they were quarried. Some quarries produced naturally-formed slabs of even thickness, known as presents, ready to be trimmed to size. Presents are hard wearing but heavy and were used as far back as Roman times. The more common type are pendles, which are slabs that have been split before being used. It was not until the 16th century that an effective method for splitting limestone to form pendles was

discovered, which made for thinner slates. Traditionally the stone was dug out after harvest, then spread over the surrounding fields and covered with turf or soil so that the sap would remain in the stone. Then at the sign of the first frost, the slaters would go out and uncover the stone so the sap within would freeze overnight and expand. This caused the slabs to split into sheets. The sheets could then be trimmed and given a peg hole before being sorted into sizes ranging from about two feet long to six inches (there are local names for each size).

Cotswold stone slates are heavy (some weigh 20 kg) as the porous stone

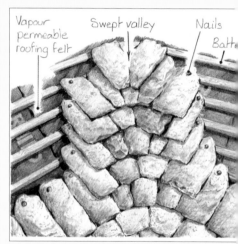

FIG 2.17: *A stone roof in the process of being laid from bottom to top with nails driven through the holes and into the battens (originally oak pegs would have hooked over them). Special cut stones are used to form the sloping corner, which is known as a swept valley. Note that about two thirds of a slate is covered by the one on top.*

FIG 2.16: *A slate or tiled roof with the larger pieces used over the wall at the bottom and the smallest at the top.*

needs to be between ½ an inch to 1 inch thick to be effective against rain, so substantial timbers are required to

FIG 2.18: ROOF TILES: *During the 19th and 20th centuries traditional roof coverings were sometimes replaced by materials from outside the region as in the above row. Welsh slate is a metamorphic rock (a sedimentary rock which has been transformed in character by pressure or heat) and produces very thin and even sheets. As these were much lighter than Cotswold stone, and had a smooth surface so rain easily flowed off, they could be set at a lower pitch. This meant the timbers could be thinner and fewer tiles were needed, making for a cheaper roof. Mass-produced clay tiles became popular in the late 19th century and they in turn were replaced after the Second World War by larger concrete tiles. If you plan to replace one of these later coverings with traditional Cotswold slates it is important to make sure that the pitch of the roof is steep and the timbers are strong enough to take the weight.*

support them. Also, because of the textured surface of the limestone, the roof has to be set at a pitch of at least 50° so that rainwater flows off and does not soak into the stone. Traditionally the edges were slanted to help them interlock but today they are usually squared off or have a 'v' shaped profile. The stones are laid from the bottom up, with the largest first as their heavier weight is best supported by the wall. The thinner, smaller stones are placed near the top. Each slate is held in place by a wooden peg, although brass or stainless steel screws and nails have also been used in recent times, and they overlap the slate below by around two thirds. Traditionally, the completed roof was torched underneath (sealed with lime mortar) so that driving rain and snow could not penetrate.

The production of pendles in the Cotswolds ended just after the Second World War and only presents are available now. However, the demand for replacement tiles or slates is growing. Old roofs need renewing after a hundred years or so, and the authorities stipulate that stone must be used. Today, much of it comes from Northamptonshire and France while artificial slates are also made. However, demand and prices are such that the sound pieces that can be removed from old roofs are very desirable.

Thatch

As a thatched roof only required material which a cottager could easily gather, like straw, reed, turf or sedge, it was common on cottages in the medieval period. It only fell from

■ LOOKING AFTER COTSWOLD STONE ROOFS

The durability of a roof depends on a number of factors as well as the general quality of the material used. The pitch needs to be correct so that water runs off and does not get absorbed causing problems when it freezes. The pitch should be at least 50° for Cotswold stone. Problems can occur when cement mortar is used for flashing and torching, as it is prone to cracking creating gaps which let water through. The amount of rainfall, sunlight and the climate local to each face will have an effect as any moisture within the stones may not evaporate making them prone to frost attack. Damage can also be caused by climbing plants and tree branches which brush against the surface while all roofs are vulnerable to careless people walking across them. Moss and lichen can be attractive but excessive amounts will hinder the drainage of rain water. Slates can also become dislodged in strong winds or when the wooden pegs fail.

It is important to check the roof regularly for faults like a dislodged or cracked slate and for problems with the ridge and flashing around chimneys. Also make sure that the verges are sound, the guttering and valleys are clear and any downpipes are not loose or cracked. If work is necessary then check that contractors are familiar with traditional methods and materials. If the whole roof is to be retiled, then breathable membranes will also have to be fitted underneath. Most roofing companies will try to retain as many of the original slates as possible as they are hard to source (it is usually the fixings, battens or timbers that fail rather than the slates themselves). As scaffolding will be required for a complete re-roofing it would be a good time to check the chimney, gable walls and aerials.

favour from the 16th century due to the fire risk and as stone slates became more widely available. Thatching was still used around the fringes of the region, especially in Oxfordshire, but with the popularity of combine harvesters after the Second World War the supply of suitable straw for roofing dried up. Of the one million thatched roofs in England in 1800, only around 35,000 still survived in 1960.

There are three types of thatched roof in England. Water reed has been traditionally limited to the Norfolk Broads and a few coastal areas where it grew in sufficient quantities. Today it is more widespread as much of what is used is imported. The finished surface is smooth with the ends flush, but the ridge section is formed out of straw as it is more flexible than reed. Combed wheat reed is straw which has been specially prepared for thatching and creates a finish similar to that of reed, but the completed roof tends to be more rounded in appearance. The long straw method uses straw which is not neatly aligned, but is laid out and

FIG 2.19: THATCHED COTTAGES: *Examples of thatched cottages in Minster Lovell (left) and Bloxham (right), Oxfordshire. In order for the thatch to throw rain off rather than have it soak through, the roof has to be at a pitch of 50-55°. Although contemporary ridges are often raised into a block form (FIG 2.20) with a shaped profile, in the past it was more usual for the ridge to be flush with the main surface of the roof. Note how the eaves are deep so that water is thrown clear of the walls below as there is no guttering. In the past the habit of sheltering under them when it was raining meant you might hear some gossip through an open window, giving us the phrase 'eaves-dropping'.*

wetted before being applied. This makes it more pliable and creates a more ragged finish with both ears and butt ends visible on the surface. These are then gathered into yealms, the bundles which are carried onto the roof to be laid. This style is usually distinguished by the lines of liggers (thin wooden rods which hold down the thatch) around the eaves and verges, rather than just the ridge as with the other methods.

A good thatch roof can last a long time without maintenance, some up to 50 years although the ridge tends to require work every 10-15 years. Water reed is more durable than straw, however, the longevity of thatching is determined more by the quality of the

FIG 2.20: THE RIDGE: *As the ridge is more vulnerable to wear than the main part of the roof it is often replaced every 10-15 years. Note the liggers holding the ridge in place.*

work, the local climate and how exposed each face is to the elements. When the surface material has rotted down or been blow away so that the sways and spars which hold each course down are becoming exposed, it is time for replacement. A water reed roof is regarded as a one-coat covering to be completely replaced when its time is up, however straw can have just its upper layer (coatwork) renewed leaving the old base in place. There are some examples of medieval thatch where this latter method has been repeatedly applied over the centuries, with the underside blackened by smoke from open fires that were burning over five hundred years ago.

FIG 2.21: A COMBED WHEAT REED ROOF BEING THATCHED: *The straw or reeds are laid from the eaves upwards with the bundles spread out over the battens and temporarily held by reeding pins (1). The surface is then dressed with a legget, a wooden bat with a ridged surface, to form an even surface (2). This is fixed by sways – metal rods in this example – held down by stainless steel wire fixed to screws driven into the rafters (3). Traditionally this was done with hazel spars or rope. The next course overhangs the previous, covering the sways until the top is reached. A ridge piece is formed and the eaves are trimmed to complete the roof. Wire netting is applied over the straw to hold it in place in exposed locations and to keep birds and vermin out, although water reed does not usually require this.*

■ FIRE

The biggest problem with a thatched roof is its vulnerability to fire. In many cases today wood burning stoves are the cause of a house burning down. This is either because sparks were created by an unsuitable fuel or the intense heat caused combustion in the chimney. Most risk can therefore be removed by only using seasoned or kiln-dried wood in a burner and ensuring that the chimney has a suitable liner. Also make sure the chimney is well maintained and that it stands at least 6ft above the ridge with a pot no greater than 2ft high. Any electrics in the loft space or bedrooms should be regularly checked as faulty wiring is another common cause of fire. Also ensure any contractor working on or near the roof has sufficient public liability insurance as the risk of fire is often greater when building work is being carried out. You can have fire retardant boards fitted under the thatch to protect the rest of the house if the roof catches fire (these need to be fitted with a suitable gap so moisture does not get trapped in the thatch). There are sprays which are designed to coat the thatch to reduce its flammability but it is not yet known how these will affect the long term performance of the roof.

FIG 2.22: CHIPPING CAMPDEN, GLOS, MODERN THATCH: *During the 19th century thatching was associated with poverty. It was only when architects in the Arts and Crafts movement sought to revive traditional materials and methods that attitudes began to change and thatch is now something of a desirable feature for the cottage owner. Today thatch is being reinstated and even included in new houses. Its use of natural materials and good insulation properties create potential for more future use.*

CHAPTER 3

Cottage Details
Windows, doors and carvings

FIG 3.1: STOW-ON-THE-WOLD, GLOS: *This row of cottages and the adjoining Victorian terrace to the left show the variety of windows, doors and fittings which can be found in the Cotswolds.*

Cottages tend to gain their romanticised image not only from their rustic walls and roofs, but also from their fixtures and fittings. Small hinged windows, planked doors and rickety chimneys were essential components of late 19th-century paintings of rural housing, and these neatly proportioned simple features are still important today for an authentic look. However, they were not originally chosen for their aesthetic appearance. Windows and doors were small because ceilings were low and budgets tight.

Before mass-produced items flooded the market in the late 19th century, these fittings were made from local materials by craftsmen based in the village or nearby town, their form reflecting the general tastes of the time but with a regional twist. The quality of these details can also tell you something about the building. For instance, a cottage with large windows, grand doorways and carved decoration was probably once a house of higher status. However, caution is necessary as many cottages have had reclaimed parts from other buildings fitted during renovations in the past century. The following

FIG 3.2: MULLION WINDOWS: *Cotswold cottages ranging from the 16th-century carved timber windows (top left) to the 19th-century ones on the bottom row. The mullions on this class of house usually had a plain chamfer while those with a carved or moulded profile were usually reserved for higher status buildings. They were universal on most cottages until the mid 18th century, much later than in most other regions. A label mould was fitted above them which kept rain out of the window opening (top and bottom centre). The short vertical pieces at the ends (label stops) prevent the wind blowing the water around the edge. By 1700 many had a single moulding running across the whole building (top right). Mullion windows were still fitted in some estate cottages in the 19th century and were later revived by Arts and Crafts architects.*

sections outline the general style of fittings used through the years. This can help in understanding a building, and in finding appropriate parts for cottage restoration projects.

Windows

Windows were originally created as much for ventilation as for bringing in light, the word coming from the Old Norse term for 'wind-eye'. Most medieval domestic windows had no glass and were divided by vertical posts called mullions to form a row of lights (the openings between the mullions), with only shutters or cloth to keep out the worst of the elements. Windows with a frame containing small pieces of glass held by diagonal lead strips which were fitted between the mullions, only became common in cottages from the late 16th century. Such was their value that glazed windows were sometimes taken by the occupant when they moved house. By the late 18th century, wooden casement windows had become common and have remained popular up to the present day. They

FIG 3.3: HOOD OR LABEL MOULDS: *Projecting along the top of mullion windows, they are a feature of 16th or 17th century Cotswold properties. They kept the rain away from the window below in the days before gutters were fitted.*

FIG 3.4: CASEMENT: *A hinged glazed frame (casement) which would have been fitted in a 17th-century mullion window. The individual pieces of glass (quarrels) were diamond shaped as they wasted less of the round spun glass used at the time.*

Stanchion.

Lead cames.

Turnbuckle catch.

Wrought iron Frame.

Handle

Stay

FIG 3.5: EXAMPLES OF CASEMENT WINDOWS: *Timber or iron casement windows became popular in the second half of the 18th century. Early examples had their lights divided by numerous glazing bars, but by the Victorian period they usually had just two or three larger pieces of glass. Estate cottages in the 19th century often had casements with elaborate ironwork imitating earlier leaded glass windows (bottom left). The weight of the wall above the window was carried by a lintel, a timber beam was common from the mid 18th century (right), a shallow arch made from stone or bricks (top left) was popular from the late 18th century especially where dressed stone was readily available. Window frames could have originally been lime washed, painted a dark colour (often unique to a country estate) or were grained to imitate a better quality wood. Brilliant white paint is a 20th-century fashion.*

were simple rectangular frames, one or two of them hinged, and divided by timber glazing bars to hold the glass. Iron windows were also popular during the 19th century. Vertical-sliding sash windows were usually reserved for larger houses, but occasionally can be found in upgraded cottages or in 19th-century terraces. Lower, horizontal-sliding sash windows were more suitable for low walled buildings. They did not require pulleys and weights so were cheaper to make.

FIG 3.6: WINDOW FITTINGS: *Casements need fittings to open and shut them. Turnbuckle catches are common in this region. They have a decorative base plate with a swivel catch to lock the window shut (left). Stays were usually a simple long iron hook, sometimes with a twisted section in 17th-century examples. Quadrant stays (right) which had a quarter circle bar of metal sticking out from the bottom of the window with a notch or thicker section to hold the window open were popular in the Cotswolds from the late 17th century and throughout the 18th. These would have originally been made of iron and were painted black.*

FIG 3.7: GLASS: *Old pieces of spun glass have a wavy texture, a green or yellow tint and contain tiny air bubbles. Where possible these should be retained when repairing windows.*

FIG 3.8: HORIZONTAL-SLIDING SASH WINDOWS: *Common in late 18th and 19th-century cottages. They are often referred to as Yorkshire sashes.*

■ WINDOW MAINTENANCE

Local conservation and listed building regulations may limit an owner's ability to replace old draughty windows with modern double-glazed units. However there are now ways of upgrading existing fittings which can meet modern energy efficiency demands without losing the valuable original appearance of the property. Local craftsmen and specialist companies can supply authentic replacements for any window not worth saving, and repair and upgrade those which are. Broken glass, snapped lead cames or rotten wood can be replaced and the layers of paint which usually make windows hard to open and close can be removed. Thin brush strips can be inserted around timber frames to save on heat loss. Modern discreet secondary glazing will not only improve energy efficiency but also help reduce noise from outside. Although cheap replacement windows may be appealing financially, they often need replacing within twenty years so repairing original fittings will not only satisfy local authorities but also save money in the long term.

FIG 3.9: DORMER WINDOWS: *They were the most popular way of getting light into the upper floor of cottages from the 17th century through to the 19th century. Most had pitched roofs (left) but they could have a hipped roof (right) which is less prominent. These often have mortar ridges which can be prone to leaking. Special shaped stones forming a swept valley were used to fill the junction between the dormer and the main roof (see FIG 2.17) which saved on using expensive lead flashing.*

FIG 3.10: *More substantial dormers could be built as part of the front wall (left). An alternative, which was popular in the Cotswolds, was to build a complete gable with a window in it (right). These tend to be half or three quarters of the height of the roof but full-height examples (sometimes on both sides of the roof) are distinctive of the weaving areas in the south and west.*

FIG 3.11: GABLES: *One of the most enduring features of Cotswold cottages are the rows of triangular gables along the top of their walls, as in these fine examples from Castle Combe, Wilts.*

FIG 3.12: COURT HOUSE, OWLPEN MANOR, GLOS: *An example of a building with a full height gable. The small oval window in its apex was a popular feature in the late 17th and early 18th century (see FIG 1.8) although this example dates from the 1620s. It was originally a banqueting house and was where the manor court was held.*

Doors

Original cottage doors were simple and plain, usually formed from vertical planks held together by horizontal battens on the inner face. The earliest of these plank and batten doors which survive on domestic properties date from the 16th century. They have wide planks of irregular width, often with just 2 or 3 across the door. By the 18th century, planks were thinner and more regular in size and in the following century they were machine cut so have very straight edges. Better quality doors could be decorated with patterns using nails or pieces of wood. Vertical strips were sometimes added to cover up the gaps between the planks. True panelled doors (with a rectangular frame and panels inserted into it) only became widely available in the 18th century and would have been found on some estate cottages or later Victorian terraces. With the revival of traditional forms of building in the late 19th and early 20th century, plank and batten doors once again became fashionable, although these tend to have edge pieces around the door, use numerous thin planks and have a small window in the top which are rare on the older doors.

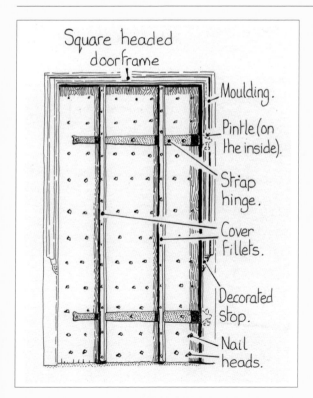

Square headed doorframe

Moulding.

Pintle (on the inside).

Strap hinge.

Cover Fillets.

Decorated Stop.

Nail heads.

FIG 3.13: A 16TH-CENTURY PLANK AND BATTEN DOOR: *Labels highlighting the details (most cottage doors would have been less decorative than this). The strap hinges were hung on pintles, vertical pins fixed into the door frame (see FIG 3.15. right).*

FIG 3.14: EXAMPLES OF PLANK AND BATTEN DOORS FROM THE 17TH CENTURY (LEFT) TO THE 20TH CENTURY (RIGHT): *Doors were originally set behind the door frame which could have a carved head or a shallow pointed arch in the 16th and early 17th century. Plainer squared-headed types were common after this. Like windows the oak door could have been left to weather to a silvery grey, or could be lime washed or painted. Green was always a popular colour.*

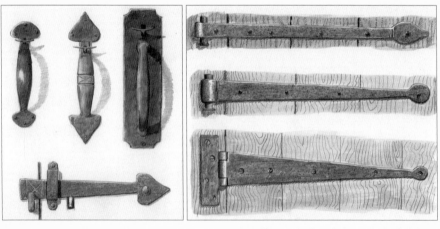

FIG 3.15: DOOR FURNITURE: *Iron rings or handles with thumb levers which lifted a latch were used to open and close a door. Strap hinges (right) were used on plank and batten doors. Early types were handmade with decorated ends on the finest (top right). By the 18th century they had a more pronounced taper along their length (centre right) and from the Victorian period they were usually machine-made with a built-in hinge (bottom right). All this ironwork would have usually been painted black.*

FIG 3.16: EXAMPLES OF PORCHES:
Porches were rare on cottages before the 19th century. There are some with a flat slab of stone held on brackets (top) usually dating from the late 17th and early 18th century, and they can be found on some estate cottages. Most examples with pitched roofs, painted timber and bargeboards (bottom) are later additions.

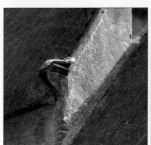  

FIG 3.17: GABLE ENDS: *In more exposed locations the end gable wall was extended upwards to protect the roof from the wind. These tend to be taller for thatch (left) and shorter for slates (centre), so if a wall looks too high for the current covering it might imply the house was originally thatched. Cotswold cottages sometimes have slate drips set into the end gable wall (right), or a line of moulded stone, to throw water clear of the vulnerable roof joint below.*

FIG 3.18: BARGEBOARDS: *These are the lengths of timber which cover the ends of a roof where it overhangs a gable end wall. Although they can be found on old timber-framed buildings most are Victorian additions. Those from the mid 19th century had the most elaborate carvings with fancy finials (left). Later ones are more restrained.*

FIG 3.19: EXAMPLES OF CHIMNEYS: *Chimneys were usually plain with a stone skirt around the base to keep rain away from the junction with the roof (left and centre). Although many are made from rubble today or repaired with brick (right) dressed blocks were originally used to limit damage from water. Limestone chimneys are vulnerable to sulphate attack which can make them lean and crack.*

FIG 3.20: THE ARTS AND CRAFTS COTTAGE: *Arts and Crafts architects used the details from old buildings to inspire new designs. Doors were simple and often featured hand-crafted ironwork, small windows and lanterns. Guttering was often held out on decorative metal brackets. The most distinctive features were mullion windows with rows of four, five or six lights. These had rectangular pieces of leaded glass rather than the diamond-shaped originals, as they were cut from flat sheets rather than spun glass discs.*

CHAPTER 4

▦ *The Cottage Interior* ▦
Don't forget to duck!

FIG 4.1: *The interior of an old cottage with a living room cum kitchen in the foreground and a parlour used for spinning in the background. All the fixtures and fittings had a practical purpose, there is little in the way of decoration or luxury.*

If today's cottage owners could step back in time and see the interior of their homes just a century or two ago they would be struck by the darkness, smell and clutter. Tools, work materials, food produce and the equipment used for cooking and washing filled the gloomy, dank interiors rather than the furniture and fittings you would find today. Inventories from old wills reveal that most had little more than a room or two with just the bare essentials of somewhere to cook, sit and sleep. There would only be a few people in a village who had acquired fixings like plate racks with their best crockery on display, larger pieces of furniture, fabric curtains or a colourful rug. Most occupants of a cottage were poorly paid tenants who worked very long hours. There was little time or money for the finer things in life. They aspired to having meat for a special meal on Sunday rather than worrying about the surroundings they ate in.

The earliest cottages would have had the main living space centred on an open fire with a pot or cauldron hanging from a hook above it. There would have been no ceiling, just the underside of the smoke-blackened roof timbers, with a table, benches or stools, and the trappings of the cottagers' line of work. There also would have been the noise and smell from any livestock housed within the building.

The major change in the interior of a cottage came through the adoption of the fireplace and chimney during the 17th century. This permitted an upper floor to be inserted, which might have been just a gallery at one end with a ladder to access it, or a complete floor with compact

FIG 4.2: THE EARLIEST COTTAGES: *This interior of a black house on the Isle of Lewis recreates the smoky, cramped conditions in medieval longhouses and basic one-roomed cottages.*

steep stairs tucked into a corner. As cottage dwellers increasingly had to supplement their incomes and take on a trade like spinning or weaving, so another ground floor room or upper storey was needed to accommodate the equipment. Furniture would have been limited, although they might have had a few chairs, built in cupboards and a chest for their belongings.

In the Victorian period there was greater variety in the housing stock for the poor. Those in estate cottages or new terraces might have had a brick or stone-flagged floor, painted walls, plaster ceilings and a cooking stove in the fireplace.

■ A SQUASH AND A SQUEEZE

It seems incredible today to think that some cottages with only one or two ground floor rooms had to accommodate a working family with numerous children and elderly relatives. The squeeze would seem even more unbearable when you remember that many had to fit in work equipment, tools and the products they made. However, it should be remembered that the family would rarely have all been in the cottage together at the same time. Many adults went straight to the local hostelry after working all day. Some chores could be done in the garden or in an outhouse, which may now have long since gone. The youngest children could play outside while the eldest would look after them, if they hadn't already been put out to work.

FIG 4.3: THE 1930s COTTAGE: *The ground floor rooms of cottages were multifunctional. The key room in any household was the living room/kitchen where most household chores like cooking and washing took place. It would have been dominated by a large fireplace and all its trappings (possibly the only one in the cottage) and there would have been a table with stools or benches, and wall cupboards, shelves and hooks for storage. If there was a second room then it would be a parlour. In the oldest cottages this would have originally been where the man and woman of the house slept while the children and relatives went upstairs. Later, it could be a space reserved for the family and guests in the evening or on Sunday, or be used for weaving, spinning and the storage of valuable goods. These cluttered rooms could still be found in the 20th century, as demonstrated by this restored 1930s interior of the Fisherman's Cottage, Clovelly, Devon.*

FIG 4.4: INTERNAL WALLS: *In many cottages the walls were no more than exposed stone with lime wash. A similar treatment was applied to the underside of the floor above, which acted as a ceiling. In 18th and 19th-century cottages plastered walls and ceilings were likely to be fitted. The plaster mix was applied directly to the exterior walls or could be spread over rows of laths (thin strips of wood) as can be seen in the ruined cottage above. Square wooden panelling was a sign of luxury rarely found an old cottage although more recent replicas or reused sections from another building can be found. Vertical wood panelling, often with a cock bead down one edge, was more common in this class of housing. Wallpaper only became affordable in the Victorian period and was found in the better class of cottage. Stencilling could have been used elsewhere as a cheaper way of achieving the same effect. Plasterboard became available after the Second World War and has replaced or covered many traditional ceilings and walls.*

If they had two downstairs rooms they may have reserved one for Sundays and special occasions and crammed everyday clutter into the living room next door. Upstairs, there would have been a couple of bedrooms with metal bedsteads and a washbasin. If there was a small fireplace in one of the bedrooms it would only have been lit when someone infirm or ill was residing there. For those less fortunate, floors might have been of beaten earth, walls rough with just a lime or colour wash coating, ceilings the underside of the floor above, and a simple grate and brick oven in the fireplace.

■ INVENTORIES

Inventories from wills and other pieces of literature from the 18th and 19th centuries can reveal much about the interior of cottages from the period. Furniture was usually limited to a small table, a few old stools or chairs, a chest or cupboard and a bedstead. Other pieces which we might expect, like dressers, are less frequently mentioned. Most had a hook to hang pots over the fire until cooking stoves became more common in the late 19th century. There were tools used by labourers and equipment like spinning wheels although large items like looms were usually not the property of the weaver. Other basic items listed include earthenware pots, occasional pieces of pewter, glass bottles, window hangings, blankets and a few sheets. It was usually a rather meagre collection for all those years of hard toil.

■ THE MODERN COTTAGE INTERIOR

Unlike the exterior where an authentic appearance is both desirable and necessary for a listed building, there is more freedom with the interior. Although in the oldest properties certain original features must be retained (check with the local authority) the owner usually has a free hand in choosing the colour, layout and fittings. A labourer's cottage had plain interiors with few of the furnishings and fittings we would now consider as essential, so there is no point trying to replicate a cottage kitchen as there are no genuine ones to base it on. Owners would be better to seek an appropriate look rather than worrying about creating an authentic structure for such rooms.

In the kitchen, built in furniture with continuous worktops are convenient but don't always suit the age of the property. Try confining them to the sink and cooker run and using some freestanding pieces, or a central table or island. Wall units can be a problem with low ceilings and close a room in so consider limiting them and using some shelving or racks to hang utensils from instead. It can be tempting to position cookers into an old fireplace but be warned you can bang your head as the space is often too low and it can make extraction difficult (it cannot be ducted up the chimney).

Heating the cottage can be a problem as gas is not always available in villages. Wood burners are effective and look the part, but make sure they are fitted correctly with suitable chimney liners (see p43). Electric heating is expensive but new storage heater systems are more efficient, reliable and better at retaining heat for the evening than the older models. Digital control panels can be set remotely so may be convenient for those who do not live permanently in their cottage. Heating by oil or gas cylinders can be more effective but has the problem of having tanks to hide. They also have higher installation and maintenance costs.

Natural wood furniture with plain and simple styled doors are always a good option. Do not be afraid to mix them up with a few pieces in different woods or styles, as the original cottage would have contained a mix of old hand me downs and second-hand pieces. The current fashion is to expose natural materials where we find them in the home. Old timber beams, stone walls and rustic brickwork are shown off and the marks, sockets and old holes found in them can be fascinating details. Avoid using oil based paint or vinyl wallpaper on walls, water based or traditional paints are now widely available and allow the walls to breathe. It is also a good idea to make sure that furniture or kitchen units are not tight up against an external solid wall. Try pulling them away a bit to allow the air to pass behind, or reposition them on an internal dividing wall. This should help reduce any potential problems with mould and damp.

Although some had first-floor sleeping accommodation, there were still many who had to use boxed-in beds against a wall in their one ground-floor room.

FIG 4.5: FLOORS: *The ground floor of most cottages would have originally been of earth. This most simple of surfaces would have been prepared by digging or raking over the surface and adding material like clay, lime, brick dust, ash and even bull's blood. This was then beaten or rammed down to create a reasonably smooth and hard surface. Straw could have been spread over the surface to collect the daily dirt and animal waste. Stone flags were desirable and could be found in some buildings we now call cottages from the 17th century, but it was only in estate cottages and later Victorian terraces where these or brick floors were common, as in the above examples. Flags had to be scrubbed clean, then washed over with milk which when dry gave a distinctive glaze to protect and seal the porous stone. In some labourers' cottages upstairs floors were nothing more than thin strips of wood (laths) nailed to joists and covered in plaster. Floorboards were not universal until the 19th century.*

■ THE PROBLEM WITH SOLID FLOORS

Solid floors were intended to allow moisture from the ground to pass through them, the passage of air and heat within the original draughty house evaporated the moisture away so it did not cause problems. In recent times, cottage owners have sealed and insulated their homes and filled them with furniture and fitted carpets which restrict the circulation of air. Many have also had the original floors ripped up and replaced with solid concrete and a damp-proof membrane so it is impermeable to water. This often causes a new problem as the moisture which formerly evaporated away is drawn up into the walls as rising damp.

Where these solid floors still exist there is the option of trying to adapt to living with them. Choose rugs without rubber backings which can allow them to breathe, use freestanding furniture with legs or castors so air can pass beneath and make sure there is good ventilation.

If the floor is in such poor condition that it needs to be replaced, then a new system using natural hydraulic lime binders can be used which allows the floor to breathe while the aggregates included in the mix improve its insulating potential.

FIG 4.6: FIREPLACES: *Fireplaces were spacious openings supported by a timber beam, stone lintel or arch (see FIG 4.1). They would have contained a simple iron grate and a small opening to one side for a bread oven (above). In some cottages an inglenook fireplace gave sufficient room for a simple bench to one side while a small cupboard built into the wall could be used for storing ingredients as the heat would have kept them dry. Coal only became widely available in the 19th century when compact cast-iron grates could be used. Today, if these old fireplaces are blocked up, make sure a vent has been installed to keep the chimney dry.*

FIG 4.7: THE RANGE: *It was not until the second half of the 19th century that simple cast-iron cooking ranges were found in cottages. This example has an open fire with a trivet above, and an oven. Later versions were closed with a hotplate and chimney above the fire. Despite their visual appeal they were hard to control and needed frequent cleaning.*

■ 'WATER, WATER, EVERYWHERE, NOR ANY DROP TO DRINK.'
Fresh water was not widely drunk in the past. It was primarily used for cooking and washing. Beer was the staple drink of the poor who drank weak brews throughout the day and stronger ones on special occasions. Tea became popular from the late 18th century although the leaves were usually second-hand, having been first used by richer folk. The brewing and boiling process not only made for a tastier drop but also removed most of the harmful elements from the water which was usually contaminated. It was not until the late 19th century that the link between illness and dirty water was made, and many villages were not connected to a reliable fresh water supply until the 20th century.

FIG 4.8: DOWNSTAIRS:
*Extensions at the rear could be
used as a pantry, scullery, or for
the preparation of food.*

FIG 4.9: UPSTAIRS: *Bedrooms
would have been simple with
just a metal bedstead, a crude
mattress and a washbasin.
There were no bathrooms.
This example from the
Fisherman's Cottage, Clovelly,
has a fireplace which would be
rare in older cottages. It would
only have been lit when
someone infirm or elderly was
sleeping there.*

CHAPTER 5

The Cottage Garden
Roses, Hollyhocks and Lavender

FIG 5.1: ARLINGTON ROW, BIBURY, GLOS: *Our image of the perfect Cotswold cottage is not complete until you add the splash of colourful flowers at the front and a backdrop of fruit trees and rich woodland.*

The cottage garden we are familiar with today is a relatively modern creation. The seemingly haphazard arrangement of colourful flowers, climbers and herbs packed into beds developed in the late 19th century. Today, at its best, it is a skilled art form designed for visual impact and traditional appearance. The real gardens which would have surrounded

FIG 5.2: WORKING GARDENS: *Most cottage gardens in the past would have appeared much like this example in Upper Slaughter, Glos. The garden was a working plot more akin to an allotment or orchard than the beautiful floral creations which are seen today.*

■ TRADITIONAL COTTAGE GARDEN PLANTS

Records from as far back as the 16th century give us some clues as to what was being grown in cottage gardens. Flowers included lavender, sweet william, primrose, violet, hollyhock, Madonna lily, corn marigold, love-lies-bleeding, and calendula. Thyme, sage, catmint, lungwort, parsley, borage, chervil, marjoram and bergamot were some of the commonly grown herbs. Vegetables, which were used to feed livestock and to add substance or flavour to simple meals, included onions, leeks, cabbage, broad beans, marrowfat peas, turnips, carrots and garlic. Apples, pears, plums, cherries, gooseberries and strawberries were also common. There are even records that hops were widely grown after the main beer producer, the monasteries, were dissolved.

most cottages up until the early 20th century were a vital source of sustenance for the family. Pigs, hens and geese would have been common, with wooden structures to keep them in. A cow was too expensive for many labourers and a horse was a rarity until much later. Fruit, vegetables and herbs were grown not only for food and animal fodder, but also for medicines, fragrances and dyes. By the 19th century more exotic plants might have also found their way into the cottage garden, often via the head gardener of the local country estate. Some people also grew flowers like dahlias and gladioli and sold them at the garden gate.

The Modern Cottage Garden

Although romanticised images of tumbledown cottages surrounded by richly-coloured flower beds and climbing plants inspired architects and gardeners alike from the late Victorian period, the informally designed garden with simple, hardy plants has many of

FIG 5.3: ALLOTMENTS: *In the medieval period it was in the interest of landowners to allocate land to even the poorest in their village in order to retain the maximum numbers to take up arms in his name. As this feudal system broke down so cottagers found land harder to come by, despite an act of 1549 which secured for them land for gardens or orchards, and another of 1589 which forbade the erection of cottages unless four acres were attached. Some people working on country estates had large gardens and allotments attached to their cottages as here at Sherborne in Gloucestershire. However, for many, the enclosure of their village left them with nothing more than a small garden plot to live off. From the late 19th century new allotments began to be created for these villagers.*

its roots in the earlier estates of the rich. Some had been experimenting with this new approach for decades. The influential garden designer Gertrude Jekyll (1843-1932) created new wild flower gardens around some of the leading Arts and Crafts houses of the late 19th century. In contrast to the flat carpet bedding of brightly coloured annuals and the exotic foreign shrubs and trees which surrounded most large Victorian houses, her designs mixed native flowers, herbs and vegetables into tightly packed beds to form an artistic creation. Nature and the gardener formed the design in tandem. One of the most influential gardeners and writers, who promoted the planting of wild flowers, was William Robinson (1838-1935). He differed from his more artistic contemporaries by advocating a less planned approach. He helped establish the cottage garden with its simpler layout of wild flowers, and with an appearance of minimal interference from the gardener. The overall effect was of rustic charm, a homely scale, and tightly packed spaces with colours which seem to have been casually thrown together.

Inspired by this, the modern cottage garden is a colourful and natural looking space. Flower beds are not only richly coloured and scented, but also closely planted to reduce the need for weeding and watering. Many prefer to coordinate colours and control the structure, while others have a more random approach and see how things develop. Flowers, vegetables and herbs grow amongst each other, with plants of a suitable scale chosen for these small spaces, and with a form and colour which suits the rural location. Plants of contrasting height, spread and

FIG 5.4: GARDEN FEATURES: *William Robinson noted that 'One lesson of these little gardens, that are so pretty, is that one can get good effects from simple materials'. Fancy ironwork, stone statues and sundials are often found but would have originally been more at home in a manor house garden than that of a labourer. Cottage garden features should be modest in size and simple in design. Drystone walls, paling fences and wicket gates are the most distinctive way of surrounding a plot. They allow plants to spread over them while rustic poles and fallen tree branches can form appropriate garden structures.*

form can be grouped together with plain foliage planted between flowers to help avoid any colour clashes.

Cottage garden plants

There is a huge choice of flowers, herbs, shrubs and vegetables which you can grow in a modern cottage garden. Old fashioned or traditional native plants are always popular, but many modern variants and imported ones can be used as long as they are hardy. The soil type, aspect and exposure to wind and frost should always be considered. Make any improvements to the soil, like adding sand to clays and removing weeds, before you start planting as this will be harder once the tightly packed plants have grown. Apart from adding light doses of fertiliser into poorer soils and mulching through the winter months, maintenance should be low. This does not have to be a precise art, part of the fun is in trying something out and if it does not work you can always soak the roots and move a plant elsewhere.

The most distinctive flower of the cottage garden is the rose, traditional types with a strong fragrance and lush foliage are the most suitable. Try Rosa gallica, Rosa centifolia, Rosa rugosa 'Rubra' and English roses by David Austin. Climbers draped over arches or scaling stone walls are also characteristic, especially clematis, honeysuckle and hollyhocks. Clematis armandii, Clematis flammula, and Lonicera periclymenum are good examples. Traditional cottage garden herbs and vegetables are still grown, while others are now appreciated for their appearance, like Cardoon,

Jerusalem artichoke, squashes, climbing beans and coloured lettuces. Small fruit trees are still popular as are shrubs like dogwood and hazel.

Some plants are good at breaking up beds of colourful flowers and have

■ SOIL ACIDITY

A good growing soil or loam is formed by fairly even proportions of clay, sand and silts. Where one of these dominates there usually has to be some compromise in the choice of plants grown. Account also needs to be taken of how acidic or alkaline the soil is as certain plants struggle if the pH is too high or low (acid is around 4-6, alkaline 8-9 and neutral 7). Simple meters and more accurate testing kits are available from garden centres and it is always worth asking neighbours for advice. If you find the soil restricts the growing of a favourite plant then one of the advantages of a cottage garden is that you can use containers and raised beds in which you can control the type of soil used. Generally across the Cotswolds the soil is lime-rich and hence alkaline, free draining and prone to nitrates leaching out which can restrict the choice of plants. Around the edges of the region the soil contains more clay and is more productive. Cranfield University has catalogued soil types across the country and you can discover more about the soil in a specific location at www.landis.org.uk.

interest in their leaves and structure, heucheras are good examples. Others are useful for attracting butterflies and bees, for instance buddleia, calendula, comfrey, lavender, catmint, marjoram, bergamot and borage. Wild flowers like meadow cranesbill, red campion, lady's smock and celandine are also popular. The largest group of plants in a cottage garden are annuals and perennials. These include pansy, sweet william, marigold, lily, daisy, crocus, delphinium, dianthus, foxglove, hollyhock, geranium, Madonna lily, Jerusalem cross, cowslip, euphorbia, lavender, evening primrose, and lily of the valley. To help narrow down this bewildering choice there are many very good books and websites which can recommend suitable flowers. The Royal Horticultural Society's website is

FIG 5.6: GARDEN TRENDS: *Unlike Cotswold cottages which display their history in stone, the gardens which surrounded them leave no such footprint. Most of what we know of their former appearance is gleaned from snippets of literature and this is often hard to interpret. It is also tricky to be sure how garden fashions would have affected the gardens of the poor, if at all. It would be wrong to assume that all cottage gardens developed along similar lines, just as today there are those who can not be bothered to do anything but the minimum while others have the time and inclination to explore and experiment. People certainly exchanged ideas and swapped seeds, but the opportunity to do so would have been dependent on so many factors, soil, climate, and aspect. Those living in an estate village may have had a permanent garden which they were encouraged to maintain, others with a more transitional lifestyle would have planted just what they needed as they could be moved on at anytime. We can only be more certain of the development of cottage gardens from the 19th century as photos, magazines and paintings, like this example by Helen Attingham, create a more accurate picture.*

FIG 5.5: AN ATTRACTIVE COTTAGE GARDEN IN CHIPPING CAMPDEN: *Although it appears to be wild it reveals the human touch in the choice of purple, mauve and pinks along with white and cream flowers, and the use of delicate and compact species.*

particularly useful as you can filter the plants for soil, sunlight and garden type. (www.rhs.org.uk/plants).

FIG 5.7: OUTBUILDINGS: *Whether down the back of a cottage or scattered around the plot, outbuildings can be of interest. The simple wooden structures used to store tools or keep livestock will rarely survive, but more substantial brick or stone buildings might, and can indicate when a trade was formerly carried out on the site. The size, form and details of the structure might help establish if it was a carpenters or blacksmiths, perhaps stables for an inn, or if they were related to the weaving industry. Old maps, black and white photos and Victorian trade directories can often help establish if a business was carried out on the site. Some urban and estate cottages had outbuildings provided along the rear, as in this row at Sherborne, Glos, which could have been for a scullery, wash room or a privy.*

FIG 5.8: BOUNDARIES: *The cottage plot would have been surrounded by either simple wooden fencing, hedging plants or dry stone walls. Hawthorn, holly, privet and elderberry were useful not just because they formed a barrier which could keep wandering livestock off the precious crops, but because they could provide flowers and fruit for drinks and ointments or timber to make poles or small wooden implements. Dry stone walls were common around estate cottages and later 19th century homes with many being built as part of the enclosure process. Although they may seem simple in form, it takes great skill and experience to create the structure. The stones are carefully selected so they interlock with the flat edges forming the outer faces and the smaller ones the inner core. A line of vertical coping stones traditionally finished the top, although many today are just capped off with mortar or cement. Sometimes a more substantial old wall bounds a cottage and this could indicate that either the property was once more important and has been divided up at a later date, or that it once stood next to an important building.*

FIG 5.9: SHERBORNE, GLOS: *Fruit trees or small orchards were once common in many cottage gardens in the area.*

FIG 5.10: THE PRIVY. *Flushing toilets were a luxury labourers could only dream of. Many cottages before the mid 20th century had far cruder facilities. Inside the house there would only have been a chamber pot for if you got caught short in the night, and this would have to be emptied out in the morning with a trek down the garden path to the privy. The privy was typically in a small stone shed with a little pitched roof. Inside would be a wooden seat with one or two holes cut into it. A few emptied out into a stream or ditch below, with the water washing out the waste. Most just had a bucket which when full would be emptied into a hole or trench dug in the garden, or was mixed with other waste to make fertiliser. In the late 19th century a popular option was an earth closet, which had a chamber above the seat. This held ash and soil to drop down over the waste when a lever was pulled. Thankfully, the irksome job of having to walk down the garden in all weathers whenever you wanted to relieve yourself is a distant memory today, although old stone privies can still be found.*

Places to Visit

If you would like to browse around beautiful villages or towns and admire cottages in their setting then the following is a list of some of the finest which have been included in this book. Please note the cottages featured are all private houses and most of the villages are small and have limited parking so it pays to plan your visit. If you cannot go there in person then just enter the postcode into Google Maps and take a virtual tour.

Bibury, Glos, GL7 5NJ: Although Arlington Row down by the river is a must-see site there are numerous other fine cottages throughout this picturesque village.

Bloxham OX15 4LY, Adderbury OX17 3LS and Aynho OX17 3BE: Three villages to the south of Banbury which, although not part of the Cotswolds, have excellent examples of ironstone and thatched cottages which are typical of north Oxfordshire and Northamptonshire.

Bourton-on-the-Hill, Glos, GL56 9AQ: Dramatically set cottages along a steep hill on the A44.

Burford, Oxon, OX18 4RG: One of the finest Cotswold towns with many old stone cottages hidden along the back streets.

Castle Combe, Wilts, SN14 7HU: Probably the prettiest village in England with a view across the bridge that will be familiar to many.

Chalford Hill, Glos, GL6 8DH: An old hillside weaving community near Stroud which is riddled with narrow lanes and scattered stone cottages. Parking is limited so best start at the bottom of the hill on the A419 and explore up the lanes (take care walking as there are few pavements).

Chipping Campden, Glos, GL55 6AJ: A must-see Cotswold town with cottages from different periods at either end of the High Street and around the back lanes.

Great Badminton, Glos, GL9 1DG: Richly coloured cottages line the High Street in this estate village, home of the famous horse trials.

Great Tew, Oxon, OX7 4DB: A small estate village in which old cottages and 19th-century estate houses blend seamlessly together. The Falkland Arms is a real step back in time.

Guiting Power, Glos, GL54 5TX: Picturesque little village around a tiny green with fine cottages.

Lower Slaughter

Lower Slaughter, Glos, GL54 2HS:
Beautifully set cottages and houses
with the River Eye running down the
main street. There are also notable
cottages and houses in the quieter
Upper Slaughter a mile to the
north-west.

Minster Lovell, Oxon, OX29 0RN:
The main street is lined with attractive
thatched and tiled cottages. To the
south of the B4047 is a Chartist
settlement with cottages and
allotments dating back to the
1840s.

Sherborne, Glos, GL54 3DH:
Remarkably intact estate village with
fine stone cottages set in large gardens
along the main street.

Snowshill, Glos, WR12 7JU: Idyllic
village set around a green and a
church and overlooking the old Manor
House with its cottage garden.

Stanton, Glos, WR12 7NE: One of the
finest Cotswold villages with some
houses dating back at least 500 years.
There are old stone and timber-framed
cottages to the south, around Stanway
and Didbrook.

Winchcombe, Glos, GL54 5LJ: This
once important town is now off the
beaten track so has retained most of
its old buildings. Notable cottages
along Hailes Street and Gloucester
Street and some fine Victorian
almshouses off Abbey Terrace.

If you would like to experience life in
a Cotswold cottage for yourself then
one of the best ways is to rent one for
a break. Although there are numerous
cottage holiday companies, some
historic cottages are in the care of
national bodies or part of country
estates. Try the following:
www.landmarktrust.org.uk
www.nationaltrustcottages.co.uk,
www.owlpen.com/cottages/holiday-
cottages

If you would like to see what life in a
cottage was like in the past then there
are a number of museums which
recreate rural life and old interiors:

Cogges Manor Farm
Church Lane, Witney OX28 3LA
01993 772602
www.cogges.org.uk
An excellent museum showing what
rural life was like in the Cotswolds in
the past and including a farmhouse
interior and gardens.

Snowshilll

Weald & Downland Open Air Museum
Town Lane, Singleton, nr Chichester, West Sussex, PO18 0EU
01243 811363
www.wealddown.co.uk
The finest collection of rural houses and cottages in the country and the best place to see what conditions were really like for cottage dwellers in the past.

Mary Arden's Farm
Station Road, Wilmcote, Stratford-upon-Avon, CV37 9UN
01789 293455 and
Anne Hathaway's Cottage & Gardens
Shottery Road, Stratford-upon-Avon, CV37 9HH
01789 204016 (The Shakespeare Birthplace Trust)
Two of the sites associated with Shakespeare which capture rural life in the late Tudor period and feature excellent cottage gardens.

Black Country Living Museum
Tipton Road, Dudley, DY1 4SQ
0121 557 9643
www.bclm.co.uk
One of the finest collections of industrial housing dating from the turn of the 20th century with interiors which capture how the working classes lived at the time.

Blists Hill Victorian Town
Ironbridge, Shropshire, TF 5UD
01952 433424
www.ironbridge.org.uk/our-attractions/blists-hill-victorian-town/
Large-scale recreation of a Victorian industrial town with small terraces and cottages from the period.

Websites
The following websites may be useful if you are trying to find out more about a specific cottage or are looking for advice with maintenance and restoration:
www.britishlistedbuildings.co.uk
www.heritagegateway.org.uk
www.english-heritage.org.uk/professional
www.spab.org.uk
www.buildingconservation.com
www.periodproperty.co.uk
www.climatechangeandyourhome.org.uk
www.thatchingadvisoryservices.co.uk
www.thecottagegardensociety.org.uk
www.rhs.org.uk/advice
www.cotswold.gov.uk

Books
Nikolaus Pevsner's *The Buildings of England* series is useful for details about individual buildings. The Cotswolds are covered by the Gloucestershire and Oxfordshire editions. **R.W. Brunskill** is a leading authority on vernacular architecture and his books, most notably *Houses and Cottages of Britain*, are always informative. If you want more information about stone buildings and how they were built then *Cotswold Stone Homes* by **Michael Hill and Sally Birch** is a very thorough and approachable guide. For those wanting to create a cottage garden could refer to **Geoff Hamilton's** *Cottage Gardens*.

Glossary

ASHLAR:	Smooth, squared stone masonry with fine joints.
BALUSTER:	Plain or decorated post supporting the stair rail.
BARGEBOARD:	External diagonal boards that protect the ends of the sloping roof on a gable. They were often decorated (most are Victorian in date).
BATTEN:	A sawn wooden support for hanging or nailing stone slates. A lath is used for old hand-cut strips.
BAULK:	A large timber beam.
BAY:	A vertical division of a house between trusses, sometimes reflected on the facade by a column of windows.
BAY WINDOW:	A window projecting from the facade of a house and usually resting on the ground.
BEAM:	A large horizontal timber.
BOND:	The pattern in which bricks are laid with varying arrangements of headers (the short ends) and stretchers (the long side) to ensure the strength of the structure.
BRIDGING BEAM:	A large beam running down the centre of the ceiling into which the joists are fixed (also known as a summer). It usually has chamfered or moulded lower edges.
BUTTRESS:	A vertical support angled up against a wall. Examples from the Arts and Crafts period tend to have a steep slope down the full height.
CAMES:	Lead work which holds the small panes of glass in a window.
CASEMENT WINDOW:	A window which is hinged along one side.
CAST IRON:	A brittle metal formed in moulds, whereas wrought iron is pliable and is heated and beaten into shape.
CHIMNEYPIECE:	An internal fireplace surround.
COCK BEADING:	A narrow vertical strip with a curved profile between the chamfered edges of tongue and groove panelling (it was formed on one edge of each plank rather than being a separate piece).
COPING:	Flat or profiled stones used to cap a wall or parapet.
COURSE:	A single horizontal layer of bricks or stones in a wall.
DAMP-PROOF COURSE:	A waterproof barrier incorporated within walls to stop rising damp penetrating the structure above.

DELAMINATION:	The splitting of slates or stones along the bedding planes.
DIAPER:	A diamond pattern formed in walls by different colour bricks.
DORMER WINDOW:	An upright window set in the angle of a roof and casting light into the attic rooms.
DRESSING:	The process of shaping stone blocks and roof slates.
DUTCH GABLES:	A gable with concave and convex quadrants and triangles.
EAVES:	The section of the roof timbers under the tiles or slates or thatch where they project over the wall.
FACADE:	The main vertical face of the house.
FINIAL:	An ornamental piece on top of a railing or the end of a roof ridge.
FLUE:	The duct for smoke from the fireplace up into the chimney.
GABLE:	The triangular upper section of wall at the end of a pitched roof.
GLAZING BARS:	The wooden or metal divisions of a window which support the panes.
GOTHIC:	Medieval architecture based around the pointed arch.
GOTHIC REVIVAL:	The rediscovery of Gothic architecture which was championed by Pugin and Ruskin and dominated building from the 1850s to 1870s.
HALF-TIMBERING:	A term for timber-framed construction. In some cases used to refer to a building with a stone or brick lower storey and timber-framed upper.
HANGING TILES:	Clay tiles hung vertically off thin strips of wood to cover walls.
HEADER:	The short end of a brick seen in the face of a wall.
HEARTH:	The stone or brick base of a fireplace.
HERRINGBONE:	Brickwork laid in a zigzag pattern.
HIPPED ROOF:	A roof with a slope on all four sides.
HOODMOULD:	Moulding in stone or brick over an arched window or door to throw off rainwater. Square ones are called label moulds.
INGLENOOK:	A wide recessed space for a fire often with seating to the sides.
JAMB:	The side of an opening for a door or window.
JOIST:	A timber, concrete or steel beam which supports the floor.
LEWIS/LEWIS HOLE:	A clever method of lifting blocks of stone without the need for external straps. A square, wedge-shaped hole which is wider inside than at the surface is made in the stone. Then a lewis, usually comprising of three metal sections forming the same profile as the hole, is inserted so that when it is lifted they lock inside in the hole and enable the block to be craned into position. The hole can be filled in after it is in place.

LINTEL: A flat beam above a door or window to bear the load of the wall above.

LOAD-BEARING WALL: A wall which has to support a load, usually referring to an internal wall which helps support an upper storey or the roof timbers.

MANSARD ROOF: A roof formed from two slopes at different angles which allows more height for a room within.

MORTAR: Used to fill gaps between stones and brick. It evens out the load and weatherproofs the wall as well as helping to hold the pieces in place. Traditionally it was made using lime but modern mortars are cement based.

MOULDING: A projecting strip of wood, stone or plaster on a wall or around an opening which has a moulded profile.

MULLION: The fixed vertical member dividing up a window. A window with a series of them is known as a mullion window.

OCULUS: A small oval window.

ORIEL: A projecting window on an upper storey.

PANELLING: Wooden lining of interior walls with vertical muntins and horizontal rails framing the panels.

PANTILES: Wavy or roughly 'S'-profiled clay roof tiles.

PEBBLEDASH: Render with small pebbles and stones thrown against it before it drys.

PENDLES: Limestone roof slates which have had to be split from larger stones by the action of frost. Although more time consuming to produce they tend to be thinner and lighter than presents.

PITCH: The angle at which a roof slopes. A plain sloping roof with two sides is called a pitched roof.

PLINTH: A low stone or brick base around a building.

POINTING: The exposed surface of mortar in a wall and the profile of the finished work. Repointing is the process of repairing damaged or worn mortar.

POST: A large vertical load-bearing timber.

PRESENTS: Limestone which can be found or extracted in the form of slates, ready to use as roof tiles.

PURLIN: A horizontal timber beam which is part of the roof structure and usually found halfway down the rafters.

QUOIN: The cornerstone at the external junction of stone or brick walls.

RAFTERS: Timbers which are set in a row along the slope of the roof with laths running across their upper surface onto which the tiles are fixed.

RAIL: A lesser horizontal timber between main posts and beams.

RENDER: A protective covering for a wall made from two or three layers of plaster or cement.

REVEAL: The sides of a recessed window or door opening.

RIDGE: The top section or capping of a roof.

ROUGHCAST: A render with small stones mixed in to give a rough texture when dried.

SASH WINDOW: A window of two separate sashes which slide vertically or horizontally.

SCREED: A mix of sand and cement used to form the upper layer of the ground floor.

SILL: The horizontal timber beam at the bottom of the wall or under a window.

SPUN GLASS: The traditional type of glass which was made by blowing a blob of glass from the end of a tube and spinning it to form a large disc. This was then cut up into smaller pieces for windows. As you can get more diamond shaped pieces out of these circles than rectangular ones, this was the shape that was usually used in windows made with spun glass. Old pieces of spun glass can be recognised by their uneven surface, slightly yellow or green tinge and from the tiny bubbles within them.

STRAPWORK: Flat bands of wood or plaster which form decorative and geometric patterns.

STRETCHER: The long side of a brick seen in the face of a wall.

STRING COURSE: A horizontal flat band or moulding running across a facade.

STUD: A lesser vertical timber between main posts and beams.

TERRACOTTA: Fine clay moulded into decorative pieces and fired. It is usually left unglazed.

TORCHING: The filling of gaps under a slate roof with mortar to make them windproof.

TRANSOM: A fixed horizontal bar in a window.

VERNACULAR: Buildings made from local materials in the regional style using methods of construction passed down within a particular area to make domestic and functional structures, as opposed to architect-designed structures made from mass-produced materials.

VOUSSOIR: A tapered stone or brick used to make an arch.

WAINSCOT: Timber lining of the lower part of a wall.

WALL PLATE: The main horizontal timber which runs along the top of the wall and under the eaves.

WEATHERBOARDING: Overlapping horizontal planks used to protect timber-framed structures from the elements or disguise poor quality construction.

INDEX

I hope you have enjoyed this book. If you have, and want to learn about others I've written, then please visit **www.countrysidebooks.co.uk**. My titles are available as softcover and eBooks.

Follow **Countryside Books** on **Facebook** and click 'Like' for the latest new titles and competitions.

Trevor Yorke

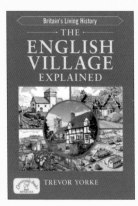

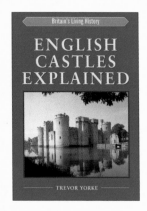

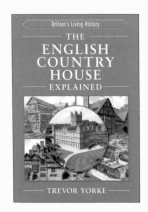

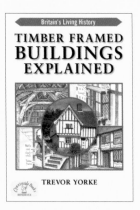

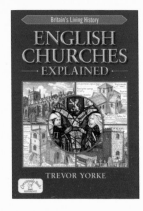